Generalizations in Historical Writing

Generalizations in Historical Writing

Edited and with an Introduction by

Alexander V. Riasanovsky
and
Barnes Riznik

University of Pennsylvania Press
Philadelphia

© 1963 by the Trustees of the University of Pennsylvania

Published in Great Britain, India, and Pakistan
by the Oxford University Press
London, Bombay, and Karachi

Library of Congress Catalog Card Number: 63-7860

The editors acknowledge the aid of The Committee on the Advancement of Research, University of Pennsylvania.

7386
Printed in the United States of America

To the memory of Professor Albert Guérard, 1880–1959, whose last written words were addressed to the future.

Contents

Introduction   11

The Historian and the Social Scientist
    H. Stuart Hughes   18

History and Theory: The Concept of Scientific History
    Isaiah Berlin   60

The Historian's Use of Nationalism and Vice Versa
    David M. Potter   114

Millennia
    Albert Guérard   167

Reflections on the Alienation of the Intellectuals
    Crane Brinton   207

Acknowledgments

We are indebted to Professors Isaiah Berlin, Crane Brinton, the late Albert Guérard, H. Stuart Hughes and David M. Potter for their contributions to this volume. Each willingly and generously agreed that any proceeds from its publication should be contributed to a Phi Alpha Theta scholarship fund.

We also wish to express our gratitude to Professors Otis A. Pease and Wayne S. Vucinich for their invaluable advice and encouragement, and to Professors Donald Lammers and Raymond A. Smith, Jr. for their comradely help.

Generalizations in Historical Writing

Introduction

By choosing his material and by arranging it into shapes and patterns, the historian creates generalizations. The act of generalizing is the historian's own contribution to the raw data of facts and figures; it is the creative dimension of historical work. The total worth of a historian is judged most frequently by the value of his generalizations. Yet, the act of generalizing all too often seems to be an unconscious one; it is taught mechanically (if at all) and performed casually, as a matter of drill or habit. The making of historical generalizations is frequently unreflective.

Recently, in a private conversation, a wise and experienced historian dismissed the whole problem by saying, "A historical generalization is anything that two historians agree upon." Although made lightly, the remark nevertheless contains a serious condemnation and challenge.

Closed or totalitarian societies force agreement upon historians, making the problem of historical generalization, at least in theory, a simple one. "Historical truth" is contained in "sacred texts," which are authoritatively interpreted. It is up to the historian to shape his writings—if not his thinking—in conformity to that processed "truth." In practice, the problem is more complex. Hierarchies of committees, commissions and agencies become mandatory for keeping the work of historians "pure" and ideologically "up to date." The penalty for making a wrong historical generalization has been enforced silence or even death.

In an open society, the problem of historical generalization is quite different. History is approached from numerous philosophical, religious, social, political and economic positions. It may be precisely because of this variety that many historians in an open society have shied away from discussing generalizations. Such discussion as there is all too often seems to rise to the rarefied altitudes of metaphysical dispute, where the historian suffocates, or to sink into the fusty atmosphere of party politics and personal prejudice, which chokes the historian. Good, and indeed excellent, history has been written without paying special attention to the intellectual process of making generalizations. A historian is a busy man. Why add yet another dimension to his already heavy burden?

Here is a paradox. In a closed society, generalizations are all-important. The historian is required to make use of generalizations, but these are imposed upon him; and he is not permitted to frame them himself. In an open society, the historian is free to formulate his own generalizations; but they are not required, and he often fails to apply them or, if he does so, to work them out with any care. This is why the statement, "A historical generalization is anything that two historians agree upon," made in the context of a free society, is both a condemnation and a challenge. It is a condemnation because historians have not in fact given sufficient conscious attention to the process of generalization-making, and thus it becomes a challenge to do something about the omission. So long as free and creative history is written, generalizations will be part of that history. It would seem worthwhile, therefore, to examine the intellectual process of generalizing on the assumption that a conscious and reflective act is better than an unreflective one.

Introduction

The five historians who have contributed to this volume chose their own topics. Thus the book as a whole is not a sequence but a cluster, in which not only the varying emphasis—here largely upon the practical and there largely upon the theoretical aspects—but also the choice of topics in itself illustrates the pluralistic nature of historical generalizations.

In the first essay, "The Historian and the Social Scientist,"[1] Professor H. Stuart Hughes raises the crucial question of exactly where and how the historian generalizes as he writes from any of the various specialized branches of historical knowledge. For Professor Hughes, generalizing starts at the very beginning with the choice of material and permeates the entire activity of investigation and presentation. The form of presentation is forged from the historian's presuppositions.

Professor Hughes goes on to suggest that the historian may engage in any or all of four major types of generalizations: "semantic aspects," "groupings of statements," "schematizations" and "metahistory." Virtually all historians, he believes, indulge in the first two kinds of generalization; most are unwilling to go beyond them. For Professor Hughes himself it is the third level, that of "schematization," which merits particular attention. "Schematization" he defines as a fitting of the pieces of historical data into the organized form, "process" or "structure." By "process" he means a coherent theory of change. By "structure" he means the interpretation of a static cross section of a particular situation in the past.

---

[1] Since being submitted for the present volume, this essay has appeared in *The American Historical Review* (LXVI, 20–46; October 1960). It was also presented at the 1959 meeting of the American Historical Association.

In his contribution, "The Concept of Scientific History," [2] Professor Isaiah Berlin combines the professional skills of a historian with those of a philosopher in discussing the problem of historical generalizations on a theoretical level. He suggests that science has achieved precision in formulating generally accepted concepts which have been operationally useful. Is there a lesson here for the historian? Without denying the value of scientific methodology, Professor Berlin finds the discipline of science (or at any rate the "science" that inspired the positivists) and history to be substantively different—not antagonistic, yet not interchangeable. Rather, he suggests, the two should complement each other in man's effort to understand his total environment. Nevertheless, he believes that the acceptance and application of scientific formulation to historical writing can be harmful. It has resulted in the curious hybrid of positivism, which, according to Professor Berlin, was both unscientific and unhistorical. Although few historians now would claim to be positivists, the influences of that attitude persist; they persist as generalizations or "maxims" which for all their beguiling promise of certainty inhibit the sensitivity for "human history." "They [historians] are told to attend to the lives of ordinary men," Professor Berlin observes, "or to economic considerations or social factors or irrational impulses or traditional and unconscious springs of action; not to forget such impersonal, inconspicuous, dull, slowly or imperceptibly altering factors of change, as erosion of the soil, or systems of irrigation and drainage, which may be more influential than spectacular victories, or catastrophic events, or acts of genius; they are told not to allow themselves to be carried away by the desire to be entertaining or paradoxical, or over-rationalistic, or to point a

---

[2] This essay first appeared in *History and Theory: Studies in The Philosophy of History* (I, 1–31; 1960).

moral or demonstrate a theory; and much else of this kind."
According to Professor Berlin, however, the historian has
his own world view to create, his human past to discover
and describe. In this quest science is not enough.

Professor David M. Potter's essay, "The Historian's Use
of Nationalism and *Vice Versa*," is an examination of the
way generalizations which are accepted in theory may
become warped in practice.[3] In theory the historian conceives of nationalism as a psychological manifestation—
a feeling of unity among an aggregate of people. As such,
this feeling is a form of group loyalty, generally similar to
other forms of group loyalty. It is an attitude varying in
degree of intensity, relative rather than absolute, functional
rather than formal. But in practice, the historian uses the
concept as a touchstone or criterion to determine whether
a given body of persons constitute a "people" and have a
right to form an autonomous state. In this sense, the concept ceases to be descriptive, and becomes a sanctioning or
evaluative idea, used to measure the validity of claims to
political autonomy. When it is used in this way, loyalty to
the nation is regarded as distinctive from other forms of
loyalty; it is conceived of as a fixed quality, categorically
existent or nonexistent in any given case, and absolute
rather than relative. Soon the historian finds that because
of his need for this formalistic index, he reverses his position and instead of measuring nationalism by the existence
of loyalty, he begins to measure the obligation of loyalty
by the existence of a nationality to which it is owed, and
he also looks for deep cultural roots to justify the existence
of a separate nationality. Potter's paper falls into two parts
—the first developing these points theoretically, the second

---

[3] Professor Potter's essay was written especially for this volume. A shorter version of it appeared in *The American Historical Review* (LXVII, 924–950, July 1962).

discussing how they have been applied in a concrete historical situation. The situation chosen is the interplay of nationalism and sectionalism in the United States during the period leading to the Civil War.

Professor Albert Guérard's essay, "Millennia," describes another dimension of the concept of nationalism. Professor Guérard's "nationalism" is not only a "schematization" of the past or present but also a projection into the future. Because the historian re-creates the past and anticipates the future, his awareness of both is retrospective and prospective. The historian—as well as the historical personality—is not only pushed by the past but drawn by the future. "Every cause, every faith, every nation exists only because it heralds a millennium," Professor Guérard writes. He believes that the most potent prospective myth is that of the "national millennium"—an idealized golden age. If there never was a France, he remarks, there was always a growing desire that France should be. It is characteristic of Professor Guérard as a thinker and a historian that in his last essay he should have directed his thoughts to the future as a help in explaining the past.

Professor Guérard's discussion makes explicit yet another historical use of generalization—the historical "myth" as distinct from historical reality. The historian's inevitable inability to re-create the past exactly as it was affords him the advantage of perspective. He can make generalizations separating what men in the past thought or said they did and wanted from what they actually did and wanted.

The structure and process of "alienation" at a critical point in the life of the intellectual class within our society is the subject of Professor Crane Brinton's essay. Professor Brinton defines the "intellectual class" as those who "teach, preach, do research in the fields of science and learning, write, compose music and pursue the fine arts, and those who regard their role as audience or followers of such persons as the most important or significant part of their lives." Professor Brinton asks two questions: What are the individual's normal attitudes toward the society, and what relation exists between the dissatisfaction of the intellectuals and the stability of society? He concludes that American intellectuals are having a much harder time adjusting themselves to the failure of their hopes for society than, for example, early Christians had in accepting the indefinite postponement of the expectation of a Second Coming of Christ. Yet as the intellectuals search for order in institutions and beliefs, Professor Brinton asserts, they are merely exercising their right to withdraw and transfer allegiance. Only if the search proves ultimately futile will there be any real "alienation." The American intellectual has, he suggests, too much at stake in things as they are to admit final desperation.

The variety of approaches by the contributors argues against any monistic attitude toward historical generalizations. However, one of the difficulties in talking about historical generalizations in a free, open society is the problem of finding a language in the middle ground between abstract speculation and mere recording of raw empirical data. These essays are a contribution to the persistent but still sporadic effort being made to show that the reflective intellectual process involved in historical generalization is useful, even if there is disagreement both on the nature of the generalizations made and on the workings of the process itself. The subject continues to invite reflection and discussion.

ALEXANDER V. RIASANOVSKY
BARNES RIZNIK

Washington, D. C.
January 1963

The Historian and the Social Scientist

H. Stuart Hughes

H. Stuart Hughes was born in 1916 in New York City. He received his B.A. degree from Amherst College and his M.A. and Ph.D. from Harvard. Before the Second World War he also studied in Europe, at Heidelberg University and the University of Munich, and worked in the Archives Nationales in Paris, where he did research on a John Harvard Traveling Fellowship. He taught history at Brown University before he enlisted in the Army as a private in 1941. By 1944 he had become chief of the Research and Analysis Branch of Strategic Services in the Mediterranean Theater; later he held the same post in Germany. He was released from active duty as a lieutenant colonel in 1946.

Since then he has served as chief of the State Department's Division of Research for Europe; as assistant professor of history at Harvard; as associate professor and as professor and head of the department of history at Stanford. Since 1957 he has been professor of history at Harvard, where he is currently directing the interdepartmental program in history and literature. He has also been a visiting member of the Institute for Advanced Study at Princeton, a fellow of the Center for Advanced Study in the Behavioral Sciences at Stanford, a fellow of the American Academy of Arts and Sciences, and the holder of a Guggenheim Fellowship.

He is the author of seven books: An Essay for Our Times; Oswald Spengler: A Critical Estimate; The United States and Italy; Consciousness and Society; Contemporary Europe: A History; An Approach to Peace; *and the forthcoming* History as Art and as Science. *He also edited* Teachers of History: Essays in Honor of Laurence Bradford Packard.

His particular fields of interest are the intellectual history of Europe during the past hundred years and the contemporary history of France and Italy.

In a number of years of teaching a graduate seminar in historiography, I have repeatedly been struck by the observation that the conventional debate as to whether history is an art or a science—whether it belongs in the curriculum with the humanities or with the social sciences—to the practicing historian makes no sense at all. As it is usually stated, this contrast implies a radical opposition, the necessity for an exclusive choice. It derives from a false notion of science and a false notion of art as two separate and logically incompatible paths to understanding.

Yet in their daily practice historians usually claim to do a bit of both. They think of their method of investigation as scientific, and of their manner of presentation as belonging to the realm of art. Thus the problem seems to be neatly solved. More closely regarded, however, this solution proves to be no solution at all. For as Benedetto Croce taught us two generations ago, in history the method of investigation and the presentation of the material—the research and the writing—are simply succeeeding (and sometimes even simultaneous) phases of the same continuous process of thought: the manner of presentation is already implicit in the presuppositions of the investigation itself.

Now this continuous process of thought is what I want to speak about in the present essay. It will serve, I think, to suggest the link between art and science, and why history necessarily partakes of the nature of both, as, indeed, do all intellectual activities that try to combine imaginative search with logical order.

Just before the Second World War the younger generation of American historians began to grow radically dissatisfied with their craft as their teachers had imparted it to them. And it was precisely on this point of the process of thought in history that their dissatisfaction manifested itself. History as they had been taught it was an intellectually invertebrate affair: it had no clear concepts and no recognized canon of interpretation. In place of these, some rather vague notions about "causes" had to suffice. Alternatively, if the word "cause" was rejected as smacking of philosophical positivism, the less offensive term "explanations" might serve, or, more weakly still, historical "factors." The only intellectual rationale to which history could lay claim was the research methodology brought to perfection a hundred years earlier by Leopold von Ranke and handed on from generation to generation virtually unchanged. As Marc Bloch was to put it, the historian's scrupulous care in ascertaining whether an event had in fact taken place contrasted painfully with the amateurishness the same historian manifested when he came to explaining it.[1]

This dissatisfaction among the young—this search for a more coherent and schematic canon of historical thought—has exploded simultaneously in two different directions. In the first place it has manifested itself in an awakening of interest in the neo-idealist tradition of historical thinking descending from Dilthey through Croce and Collingwood, and in the more recent critiques of this tradition embodied in the short studies by Walsh, Gardiner and Dray.[2] In the

---

[1] Marc Bloch, *Apologie pour l'histoire ou métier d'historien* (Paris, 1952), translated by Peter Putnam as *The Historian's Craft* (New York, 1953), 195.

[2] W. H. Walsh, *An Introduction to Philosophy of History* (London, 1951); Patrick Gardiner, *The Nature of Historical Explanation* (Oxford, Eng., 1952); William Dray, *Laws and Explanation in History* (Oxford, Eng., 1957).

second place it has produced a new awareness of social science and of its relevance for historical study. It is more particularly of this latter manifestation of interest that I want to treat in the present essay. But as the analysis proceeds, I think it will become apparent how intimately the second interest is in fact related to the first.

Indeed, the same individuals among the younger generation of American historians have very frequently engaged their efforts in both directions at once. They have been equally concerned with social science and with the analytic philosophy of history. But to date this common interest has produced little in the way of systematic treatments. The mainstream of analytical writings on the nature of history has come from England rather than from the United States —and these have reflected the characteristic British hostility to (or perhaps, ignorance of) the claims of the social sciences. In our own country the historian's expression of interest in these fields has not gone much beyond the stage of programmatic discussion.[3] The precise points of intersection between history and the social disciplines have still to be defined.

The purpose of the present essay is to suggest how a beginning can be made in this direction. It is based on two major assumptions. First, there is the one already stated, that the historian's search for philosophical grounding and his reaching out for contact with the social sciences are complementary and related manifestations of the same quest for precision in historical explanation. Second, there is the conviction that this quest springs from an overwhelming and unprecedented intellectual confusion characteristic of the present time. During the two generations prior to the

---

[3] See, for example, the two useful reports by the Social Research Council, *The Social Sciences in Historical Study* [SSRC Bulletin No. 64] (New York, 1954); "A Conference on the Social Sciences in Historical Study, June 20–22, 1957" (mimeographed 1957, Stanford, Calif.).

Second World War, the scope of historical study grew enormously, both in this country and abroad. Economic, cultural and psychological aspects of the past were added to the politico-military emphasis which—again a legacy from Ranke—had once reigned supreme. Politics, and more particularly foreign policy, had traditionally provided the central core around which the other historical manifestations grouped themselves: it furnished a rough-and-ready principle of order for the historian's marshaling of his data. But with the admission of so much new data, much of it unmanageable in terms of the customary procedures, the familiar framework cracked. Chaos threatened—a warfare for supremacy among the different specialized branches of historical knowledge, economic, social and the like, with the probable outcome a flabby sort of truce in which the equal (and largely unrelated) claims of all were to be given equal recognition. In this situation of intellectual confusion and unparalleled heterogeneity of interpretation, a new principle of order was urgently required.

Obviously this ordering of data can arise only through generalization. And hence the problem of where and how the historian generalizes has established itself as the central one in assessing not only the claims of social science but also the canon of historical interpretation in its broadest sense.

Traditionally historians have adopted two radically different attitudes toward the problem of generalization. And this cleavage has roughly paralleled the controversy between philosophical idealism and positivism in historical study. On the one hand, historians have commonly dealt in high-level generalizations: they have introduced or concluded the individual sections of their labors with abstract reflections of a cosmic or moral character. Usually, although not necessarily, this attitude of confident generalizing has been associated with the idealist urge to trace the workings of "spirit" or "idea" through human institutions and to discern a guiding thread in historical change. In the opposite camp, historians have stressed the search for the minutiae of past events and the necessity for verifying the data at all stages of the investigation: they have been obsessed with the particular and the strictly factual. This latter attitude obviously has much in common with philosophical positivism; it emphasizes the scientific character of the historian's method while eschewing any explicit metaphysical grounding. Yet we should bear in mind that it was Ranke the idealist who first codified the methodology of the historian's craft and that it was historical positivism (of the Buckle variety) that originally undertook to discover the "laws" of historical development. These crisscrossings may serve to remind us of the extent to which historians in both the major philosophical camps have faced similar problems in the intellectual ordering of their data.

Indeed, throughout the past century the characteristic attitude of the historian has been surprisingly uniform. He has done two things at once—he has generalized in sweeping fashion and he has given almost compulsive heed to the minute details of his account. Thus this account has tended to oscillate wildly between extremes: at one time it has soared into airy generalities; more frequently it has jogged remorselessly from one detail to the next. Between the two there has been little in the way of tentative synthesis or middle ground.

It is this middle ground that currently needs to be defined. And the way to do so is through drawing distinctions among the different levels of analysis on which the historian is in fact accustomed to operate. If we can reach clarity on the nature and uses of the various levels of generalization that are available to us, then the first part of our task will have been accomplished.

And so to the debate with the social scientist. The latter quite legitimately questions: "What principles hold true (e.g., as in physical evolution) for mankind historically?" or perhaps, "How can the generalizations of social science be applied to history?" To this the historian customarily answers: "There is no such thing—history deals only with *individual* situations."

Why this failure of minds to meet? Why is the historian so reluctant to admit to his colleague in the social sciences that he does in fact engage in generalization? I think that there are two explanations, the first of which is in itself historical.

I have already recalled the overwhelming influence of Ranke and his school on subsequent historical scholarship. It has been of capital, if perhaps "accidental," importance that the leading tradition in modern historiography was established in Germany in an atmosphere dominated by the individualizing tendencies of the romantic movement. The foundation of contemporary historical scholarship thus overlapped and partly coincided with the romantic revolt against the eighteenth-century cult of general principles. And the emphasis on the individual and on the unique has remained characteristic of nearly all historians, even those who, like most contemporary Americans, reject either overtly or by implication the idealist metaphysic associated with the original tradition.

On top of this, as I have already suggested, the neo-idealist current exemplified in the work of Dilthey, Croce and

Collingwood has been particularly influential on the younger historians of the past generation. The effect has been to reinforce the original precepts of the German school. Or, more precisely, it has been to soften the blow of self-criticism in this one particular spot. For here the job already seemed to have been done. The neo-idealists had themselves, in the course of their main labors of rescuing historical study from the grip of positivistic pseudo science, tidied up what was naïve and outmoded in the original tradition. And this impression of a task already accomplished was reinforced by the fact that the older generation among American historians had not paid much attention to Dilthey and his heirs. Hence it seemed more than ever apparent that in the analytical or critical philosophy of history the main job that needed to be done was simply to introduce the wisdom of Germany, Italy and England to the New World.

Now Dilthey and his successors performed an immensely useful task in clarifying more adequately than had ever been the case before the philosophical criteria of historical study. But they failed to see that in reacting as strongly as they did against the positivist equation of history with natural science they had thrown out the baby with the bath. Croce, whose position was more extreme and coherent than Dilthey's, in effect eliminated the key concepts of "causes" and "laws" from historical explanation.[4]

This positivist-antipositivist controversy, which shook the universities of continental Europe from the 1890's to the 1920's, reached the United States in only muffled form. In America, as in England, historians generally have adopted

---

[4] On this whole subject, see my *Consciousness and Society: The Reorientation of European Social Thought, 1890–1930* (New York, 1958), Chap. VI.

a highly pragmatic attitude toward their work and have been uninterested in epistemological or methodological polemics. Hence most practicing American historians have been neither positivists nor antipositivists in any explicit sense. By and large they have retained the concept of "causes," while rejecting the idea of "laws." Thus the dominant attitude in American historical writing has been a kind of residual or truncated positivitism. Uncharitably regarded, it seems to possess the virtues neither of the positivist nor of the idealist position. From the positivists, it has kept only the insistence on the painstaking and thorough investigation of "facts": its notion of "causes" is usually even more summary and unexamined than theirs. At the same time, in rejecting the idea of "laws," it has abandoned the positivists' aspiration to find in history a structure of widely inclusive explanations and to establish it as a sister discipline in close relation to social science. In similar fashion, most American historical writing has displayed little of the imaginative sweep and philosophical sophistication associated with the idealist tradition.

The second explanation for the American historian's reluctance to generalize is both temperamental and terminological. It springs from his unwillingness to make distinctions and his tendency to treat his problems as all of a piece. In his obsession with the principle of individuality, he has failed to realize that the use of generalizations in historical writing can be, and customarily is, on radically different planes, where differing criteria of judgment apply. I think we can distinguish four of these planes. They may be characterized in terms of semantic aspects, groupings of statements, schematizations, metahistory.

Semantic aspects are the simplest and commonest form of generalization, one in which all historians indulge, even when they are unaware of it. Generalizations of this primitive type are simply built into historical language in the form of verbs or nouns (i.e., verbs like "revolutionize" or nouns like "nation"). We need elaborate this point no further: the writing of history would be totally impossible unless historians were willing to imply generalizations and abstractions from reality by using grouping words of this sort.

Groupings of statements about events are generalizations that commonly occur in the topical sentences of the paragraphs of historical writing, or, in more abstract form, in the "conclusions" of a chapter or book. Although the authors may not be entirely aware of it, such groupings of statements *always do violence* to any one historical reality. Yet the more conservative historians find this kind of statement perfectly "respectable" and unobjectionable from the standpoint of technical method.

At the same time generalizations of this second type nearly always lack explicit recognition of the assumptions on which they are founded. Let me take an example from Gardiner, who is quoting a basic French history text: " 'Louis XIV died unpopular . . . having caused France to lose . . . the incomparable position she had gained by the policy of the cardinals [that is, the great King's predecessors].' " [5] This statement obviously contains a number of assumptions about history, the French people, social psychology and the like. Let us look at a few of them: there was a kind of public opinion in France in the late seventeenth and early eighteenth centuries; this public opinion expected the ruler of the country to advance the national ranking within the European state system; it was

---

[5] Gardiner, *Nature of Historical Explanation*, 65. This example, which is repeated by Dray, is apparently becoming a minor classic in the field.

satisfied by the achievements of Louis XIV's predecessors; it was similarly disappointed when the Sun King failed to accomplish the same things. The listing could in theory go on almost indefinitely.

In actual practice, however, historians customarily restrict the groupings of statements of this sort to as limited a range as possible and refrain from spelling out their implications or their relationship to other possible generalizations. Thus, in the above example, the author is not interested in suggesting what Louis XIV's unpopularity implied for popular psychology in general, nor the relationship of his own statement to other theories of political rule, of elites, of economic class and of social status. In short, when historians generalize in this second sense, they do it as unself-consciously and over as narrow a range as possible. But the wider implications are there just the same.

Virtually all historians indulge in these first two types of generalization. Most are unwilling to go beyond them to the two types that I should now like to outline.

A schematization is a fitting of the pieces of historical data into an organized form in terms of process or structure. By process we usually mean a coherent theory of change through time as implied in such words as "industrialization" or "urbanization." By structure we suggest a more static cross section of a particular situation in the past. On this third plane the procedure of historical generalization is close to that of social science. The order of business, however, is reversed. A social scientist states a generalization for which history is expected to supply data or examples. A historian works the other way around: for him a generalization serves as a possible organizing principle to be applied to the specific series of events with which he is concerned.

In general, historians have been rather wary of this third plane. Yet a number of highly "respectable" ones have made distinguished contributions of the schematic sort: Marc Bloch's study of feudalism is a case in point.[6] Even if it is true that we rarely find complete works written on the level of schematization, it is easy to cite individual chapters or sections of books in which historians have proceeded in this fashion.

Onto the plane of metahistory—the plane on which Spengler, Toynbee and the other creators of all-inclusive systems have operated—almost no self-respecting historian will venture. My own view is that my colleagues have been far too cautious about exploring the suggestions developed on the level of metahistory. They have usually restricted themselves to a kind of literal-minded demolition, which is too easy to be particularly profitable. Once we go beyond this negative task, we discover that books of metahistory possess enormous value for the historian as imaginative reconstruction and poetic suggestion.[7] I might even go so far as to say that the metahistorians, who are alone in a position to give free play to their speculative propensities, are the writers who actually operate on the "frontiers" of historical thinking. Their theories are seldom empirically verifiable: they are much too far removed from the precise data of historical events and they are much too heavily freighted with assumptions and variables. But as imaginative hypotheses they offer the indispensable raw material for subsequent criticism and elaboration.

In terms of the distinctions that I have drawn among these four planes, I think we can now shift to the more

---

[6] Marc Bloch, *La société féodale* (2 vols., Paris, 1939).
[7] See my *Oswald Spengler: A Critical Estimate* (New York, 1952).

polemical question of how the historian's reluctance to generalize in an explicit fashion may be at least partially overcome. In a word, I suggest that historical generalizations need to be made more inclusive, and at the same time more explicit and precise. The way to do this is to begin shifting the emphasis from the second plane—mere groupings of statements—to the third plane—the level of schematizations. In such an endeavor we must be careful to explain at every stage what we are about. For I am convinced that much of the historian's nervousness springs from his unfamiliarity with this third level. When one talks of generalizing more extensively, the historian fears that one is advocating a direct leap from the second to the fourth plane, that is to the realm of people like Spengler and Toynbee, while he may not even suspect the existence of the schematic plane.

At this point, it is time to return to the terms "cause" and "law," which, as we have seen, Croce and his fellows tried to bar totally from historical discourse. My own view of the matter is that a general or "covering" law (to use Dray's expression) and an exhaustive causal explanation are alike logically impossible. At the same time I contend that the only way to make a satisfactory approach to the problem of generalization in history, and the related question of history and social science, is to restore both these concepts to the historian's vocabulary.[8] And in so doing I think we should take another look at the sharp distinction ordinarily drawn between them. On closer inspection I believe we shall find them to be intimately related. For any coherent explanation in terms of cause suggests a law-

---

[8] Dray's position (as, for example, on p. 78 of his *Laws and Explanation in History*) is actually similar to mine, but this similarity is obscured by his insistence on caricaturing the arguments of others through his "covering law" model.

ful universe: in rather summary fashion, a causal explanation may be considered as simply an example of the operation of a more general law.

An essential initial step, then, toward more confident generalizing in historical writing is to define the concept of "cause" with greater precision. A moment's reflection will suggest that all historians use some form of this concept even when they do not explicitly recognize it. (The very employment of the word "because" immediately gives warning that causal explanation is at hand.[9]) When historians (like Croce) say that they are "explaining" rather than using the category of cause, they are simply engaging in semantic obfuscation: it was one of the great strengths of the recent SSRC bulletin on history and the social sciences to have recognized this confusion.[10] It is high time that the term be reinstated (as against the idealist position) and at the same time be refined, narrowed in its range, and employed in more skeptical fashion (as against American residual positivism). I should like to elaborate on this statement in three respects.

In the first place, causal reasoning is obviously based on the assumption that human behavior is just as lawful as events in the realm of nature. Whether or not the workings of the universe are in any ultimate sense lawful is a metaphysical question, which scientists of all sorts usually an-

---

[9] It is obvious that I differ from Croce and Collingwood—and even a more moderate writer like Gardiner—in refusing to accept their distinction between the search for "laws" and the ascription of motivation, between "cause" and "because." Dray's view (*ibid.*, 151–53) is again similar to my own, except where he shows a complete (and characteristic) misunderstanding of the insistence on the part of such sociologists as Max Weber and Talcott Parsons that an action can be viewed scientifically *from the standpoint of the actor* as well as from the more usual standpoint of the observer (*ibid.*, 140: "When we subsume an action under a law, our approach is that of a spectator of the action.").

[10] *Social Sciences in Historical Study*, 86–89.

swer pragmatically by assuming that it is so. Or, in more precise terms, they explain that in the study of man, as in the natural sciences in their twentieth-century form, what we call "laws" are not strict and universal causal generalizations in the old sense, but are simply observed regularities expressing themselves as statistical probabilities. In this contemporary usage there is no radical distinction between the two fields of knowledge.[11] Indeed, we may surmise that if Croce had been acquainted with the concepts of cause and law in their more skeptical twentieth-century form, rather than in the dogmatic nineteenth-century form which was all that he knew, he might not have felt obliged to discard them in so cavalier a fashion.

Most contemporary historians, however, have followed Croce and the German idealist tradition in distinguishing human activity as a "realm of freedom," as contrasted with the "realm of necessity" characteristic of the natural world. This attitude, flattering as it may be to the individual's sense of his own uniqueness, has about it a mystical flavor, which obscures the real issue. If human behavior is capable of rational explanation at all, clearly there must be something lawful about it. Indeed, and this Max Weber was one of the first to emphasize, man never feels so free as when he is acting rationally. The essential difference, Weber asserted, between the natural and the human world was that in the latter case it was impossible to arrive at laws which would in any sense give a complete or exhaustive explanation of even the simplest human action.[12]

---

[11] Hans Reichenbach, "Probability Methods in Social Science," *The Policy Sciences: Recent Developments in Scope and Method*, ed. Daniel Lerner and Harold D. Lasswell (Stanford, Calif., 1951), 121–28.

[12] *Max Weber on the Methodology of the Social Sciences*, tr. and ed. Edward A. Shils and Henry A. Finch (Glencoe, Ill., 1949), 78, 124–25. On this whole subject, see also my *Consciousness and Society*, 296–314.

As a result, and this is the second point I should like to stress, the most satisfactory type of causal explanation in history simply tries to locate the factor which, when removed, would make the decisive difference in a given sequence of events—that is, the factor which, if thought away, would render the events in question inconceivable. Obviously a procedure of this kind suffers from all sorts of drawbacks. At the same time, if rigorously carried out, it offers more precision than any other type of causal explanation in common use among historians.[13] Its unavoidable limitations lie of course in its subjective origin: to speak of a given historical factor as decisive means to call it such from no more than one particular standpoint (that is, ultimately, from the standpoint of some value system).[14] Hence from another standpoint the events previously marked out as of controlling importance might not seem decisive in the least. What may rank as a satisfactory explanation for one person may for another be no explanation at all.[15]

Finally, the above procedure implies the possibility of running alternative causal sequences based on alternative criteria of importance, as Weber did in classic fashion in his studies of capitalism and religion. In this case, however, a word of warning is in order. The neatness and elegance of Weber's treatment—the clear-cut fashion in which he set economic and "spiritual" explanations against each other—has obscured the complexity of the procedure as it usually presents itself to historians. Weber simplified his problem by choosing to deal with only two variables. More

---

[13] Compare Dray's statement (*Laws and Explanation in History*, 105–106): "The judgment that a certain condition was crucial (both necessary and important) . . . is the standard historical case."

[14] *Max Weber on the Methodology of the Social Sciences,* ed. Shils and Finch, 166, 180–81.

[15] Dray, *Laws and Explanation in History,* 74.

commonly, historians are obliged to reckon with many more. And these are frequently of a radically incommensurable nature. Only a kind of sleight of hand can bring them to fit together.

At the same time, this incommensurability does not mean that they are mutually exclusive or necessarily incompatible. Once again it all depends on the individual historian's focus of interest. Thus an event like the outbreak of the First World War can be explained in several different and complementary ways. It is not necessary to argue endlessly over whether immediate diplomatic events or more sustained imperial rivalries or the intensification of nationalism in popular psychology or the development of capitalism into its "highest stage" was the "basic" cause. From one point of view or another, any and all of these explanations can lay claim to historical "truth."

So much for the matter of law and cause. The foregoing treatment is by no means meant to be an exhaustive survey of what may well be the most vexed point in the historian's whole conceptual apparatus. It is intended simply as a kind of reconnoitering of the ground—a summary of where the best recent studies in the analytical philosophy of history currently situate the problem. What may look like a long digression is in fact the logical approach to the question that primarily concerns us. We are interested above all in the third plane of historical generalization—the level of schematization, as I have called it. And my polemical purpose has been to justify and to further the development of historical study on this plane.

Now without some clear concept of law and cause in history—without the acceptance by the historian of the scientist's basic assumption of a lawful universe—the notion of schematization would make no sense at all. It would amount to no more than an arbitrary game, to be played by each historian as his fancy dictated. Without some grounding in an agreed on and communicable concept of cause (however much historians might disagree on individual criteria of importance), the labors of the schematizers could lay no more claim to validity than those of the metahistorians. This Weber clearly realized, and his device for coping with the problem has likewise become classic. In an effort to broaden and to generalize the causal procedure he had earlier defined, he coined the term "ideal type" to describe the sort of explanatory construction that brings order into a vastly complex body of material. As a conscious abstraction from reality—as a procedure by which a series of phenomena can be shorn of their more eccentric features and hence made comparable to other historical manifestations—the procedure of ideal-type construction is approximately the equivalent of what I have called schematization.

Here, then, we finally come to grips with the question of how the concepts of social science may be applied to historical study. Let me emphasize once again that they can properly figure neither as complete causal explanations nor as general laws. They may be applied, rather, as ideal types, or, more generally, as hypotheses of varying degrees of range and explanatory power and in a relationship of varying degrees of complementariness or contradiction to each other. For example, the central question of historical interpretation in the idealist tradition has been the ascription of motives to the leading actors in the events of the past. Customarily this has been done by some sort of "intuitive" or introspective procedure. Psychoanalytic theory offers a more coherent set of explanations, with which historians are just now beginning to reckon.[16] In this classic area of what the German idealists call inner "understanding" (*Verstehen*) the application of Freudian and post-Freudian theory might well result in a wholesale revamping of conventional notions of historical motivation.

I have mentioned psychoanalytic theory as one possible example. Social scientists could find innumerable others. In brief, my contention is that by applying mutually interdependent generalizations of varying degrees of probability, drawn from the social sciences, with no one of them considered either exhaustive or exclusive, historians can begin right now to refine and to make more explicit their whole procedure of explanation.

Moreover, the discussion thus far has, I think, considerably clarified the relation between history and social science. While no radical dissimilarity in intellectual goal has emerged, we have found a very important difference in traditional procedure. The whole line of argument has presupposed that history will remain in its original literary tradition. It has further implied that historians will continue to draw up imprecise "explanation sketches" rather than to employ the narrower and more rigorous methods of social science.[17] I should hasten to add, however, that this looser sort of procedure is by no means necessarily "unscientific." It can become perfectly acceptable as social science if, on the one hand, historians are quite conscious of their own imprecision, and if, on the other hand, social scientists recognize that the "explanation sketches" devised

---

[16] More particularly William L. Langer in his epoch-making presidential address to the American Historical Association, "The Next Assignment," *American Historical Review*, LXIII (Jan. 1958), 283–304.

[17] See Gardiner, *Nature of Historical Explanation*, 91–97, quoting Carl Hempel.

by their historical colleagues are impressionistic and require much subsequent "filling in"—that they are not susceptible of dramatic validation or invalidation, in the manner of scientific hypotheses in the classic mold, but are rather to be considered as rough outlines subject to very gradual establishment or discrediting. Should the social scientists insist that historians abandon this loose type of procedure, I do not think that the result would be better history. It would simply be a narrower kind of historical writing lacking the range and flexibility of the historian's craft as it has traditionally been practiced.

At the same time the manifest (and justified) reluctance of historians to abandon their literary affiliations is no reason why they should not try to be more explicit about what they are doing and to attempt a number of things that they have traditionally avoided. Historians, as we have seen, have always made generalizations of one sort or another. At one time these grand hypotheses were drawn from theology; more recently they have been drawn from notions of "human nature" or "common sense." In past eras historians of a philosophic turn of mind exploited the most stimulating fund of generalizations that were currently available; it has been only in the last two or three generations that they have come to distrust the findings of co-workers in other fields. And yet within this same period the social sciences have been developing to a point where it is now possible to find in them a wide and varied range of hypotheses fully capable of historical application. Under contemporary conditions, these would seem to offer the natural reservoir on which the philosophically minded historian might draw.

And so the imaginary debate with the social scientist may be provisionally settled in the following fashion: since history has no generalizations of its own—since the only specifically historical category is that of time sequence—it must necessarily borrow its intellectual rationale from elsewhere. As yet, and for the foreseeable future, neither historians nor social scientists have been able to agree on generalizations of a universal explanatory power. Indeed, the characteristic mistake of the metahistorians has been to hurry this process. There is no reason, however, why the range of generalization cannot gradually be widened so as to build out from schematizations or ideal types a bolder and more closely interlocking fund of explanations in terms of process and structure.

Now a bald assertion that a certain amount of social science theory can profitably be exploited for the purposes of historical explanation obviously requires much explanation of its own. It is not enough simply to state that this applicability exists; it is necessary to show, if only in fragmentary fashion, the approximate range through which such novel procedures can operate.

The first clarification, then, that I owe my readers is to explain once and for all that by "application" I do not mean any mechanical or one-to-one superimposing of social science theory on traditional historical prose. This is the commonest and most persistent misconception that dogs the trail of those of us who argue for closer relations between history and its sister disciplines. Once we begin to contend that the historian can profit by the example of the social scientist, we are almost sure to be accused of "selling out" to the professional enemy.

Here again the example of psychoanalytic theory may serve to illuminate the whole debate. Obviously the historian who wants to make use of the work of Freud and his successors is not obliged to give equal credit to everything they ever wrote: there is no need for him to swallow without discrimination the whole corpus of Freudian and post-Freudian writings. He may pick and choose. Indeed, there is no other sensible course when we are confronted with such a vast heterogeneity of theory, only part of which is susceptible to historical application at all. Thus the historian may well find that concepts like "projection" and "sublimation" are exactly what he needs to guide his account, while the notion of a "primal crime," as expounded in Freud's later and more speculative writings, is simply too fantastic to be considered. (Yet I might add my own impression that American cultural anthropologists have become far less scornful of *Totem and Taboo* and its sequels than they were a generation ago.)

Moreover, very frequently the word "application" is too immediate and concrete to describe accurately what the historian may most profitably do with the insights of his fellow workers in the social sciences. In many cases, perhaps in a majority of cases, he does not really "apply" them at all. He lets them remain in the back of his mind, without bringing them explicitly into the foreground of his historical writing. He does not parade his knowledge of social science theory: he simply permits his thoughts to be informed by it. This sort of process is approximately what people like Sorel and Croce had in mind when they said that Marxism would serve to "illuminate" the course of historical reasoning, long after its specific teachings had been refuted, "well-digested," or put aside. It is what a more recent theoretician of history means when he speaks of a "factor" that is worth the historian's while "to be on the lookout for." [18] A process

---

[18] Hughes, *Consciousness and Society*, 87–89; Dray, *Laws and Explanation in History*, 108.

of this kind subtly alters the character of a historian's work in ways that even the writer himself may be unaware of. To the unpracticed eye, his prose may remain just as untheoretical as in the past. But the new type of knowledge he has absorbed will actually have worked subterranean alterations in his whole mode of thought and expression: his choice of vocabulary and his explanatory line will be different, even though the cast of his prose remains irreproachably literary and discursive.

A second clarification has to do with the relative congeniality for the historian of the different social science disciplines. Some are clearly more adaptable than others to the uses to which the historical scholar would like to put them. My own impression—derived from a stay at the Center for Advanced Study in the Behavorial Sciences, which is currently providing an invaluable experience in mutual education for both social scientists and historians—is that the various disciplines rank on a fairly apparent scale of applicability, with experimental psychology at one end and cultural anthropology at the other.

Experimental psychology I have found to be the least adaptable to the historian's purposes. Its rigorous criteria of evidence and the narrowly defined level of abstraction on which it operates contrast so sharply with history's loosely metaphorical procedures as to provide almost no points of contact. At the other end of the scale, I have found cultural anthropology congenial in the extreme. Indeed, the approach of the cultural anthropologist so closely resembles that of the historian as frequently to seem identical with it. Like the historical scholar, the student of exotic cultures adopts a highly permissive attitude toward his data; he is perfectly happy in the realm of imprecision and of "intuitive" procedures; and he tries to grapple with what he regards as the central problems of the societies with which he is concerned. In this last respect, the cultural anthropologist, so the historian thinks, offers a welcome contrast to the dominant temper among his colleagues in the other social sciences. More and more the sociologists, the economists and the political scientists seem almost exclusively absorbed with the sort of small, neat topics that alone are capable of being dealt with in a methodologically impeccable fashion.

It is with these that we come to the real point of difference and debate. And it is more particularly with respect to the newer mathematical methods that the final and most important clarification of my argument is called for. The vast development of mathematical "model building" that has characterized American social science since the end of the Second World War presents a more acute problem for the historian than was true of social thought in its older and more discursive form. The lessons of Weber or Durkheim or Freud confronted history with no overwhelming intellectual difficulty. These were still couched in language close enough to the literary tradition to permit their fairly rapid absorption into the canon of historical thought. A mathematical model, however, offers a challenge of quite a different sort. In its substitution of symbols for words, its insistence on precise definition at every stage, and the closed and unequivocal character of its conclusions, it seems to fly in the face of more than two millennia of historical practice.

Thus the historian like myself who makes a point of adopting a conciliatory attitude toward the social sciences may find himself in this respect no farther advanced than his conservative colleagues. More than once when speaking in terms that I regarded as sympathetic to social science, I have found myself brought up short by the objections of my new friends. "It is all very well," they would in effect reply, "to accept Weber and the rest. But this sort of thing is now old-fashioned. You are two generations out of date."

Now a reception of this sort is quite likely to make the historical convert to social science regret that he ever made any advances at all. The natural reaction is to beat a dignified retreat to his familiar encampment. Or he may simply decide to laugh at model-building as a quite impossible aberration of the social science mind. Between ridicule of the innovators and capitulation to them no middle course seems to offer itself.

Actually there is such a course, but it is a difficult one to chart. Initially we may ask of historians that they begin to learn something of mathematics, statistics and symbolic logic—subjects of which nearly all of them, even those, like myself, who regard themselves as of a younger generation, are almost totally ignorant. Then at least they would know what they were talking about when they argued for the acceptance or rejection of techniques of this sort. Beyond that we might ask of them that they keep an open mind toward the possibilities of quantification, that they do not reject the notion of number as necessarily and by definition incompatible with the historian's craft. This is a topic on which I shall be enlarging very shortly. Meanwhile I should like to say a word on some of the more general and philosophical problems that the confrontation of the historian with mathematical social science brings to the fore.

I have stated earlier my conviction that history would cease to be itself if it deserted the literary and discursive mold in which its original practitioners cast it. By this I do not mean to suggest that such a "loose" approach is necessarily the best or only one for the discussion of human affairs. Quite the contrary. The very diversity of the attacks on similar bodies of data that history and the social sciences offer—the possibility of flanking movements and cross fires that such diversity provides—these are our best guarantees against partiality toward some aspects of social reality and the neglect of others. Philosophical pluralism is almost second nature to the practicing historian, and he sees virtue in a situation in which intellectual variety is preserved. Similarly he has a particular concern for historical origins: he delights in the richness of the past as it reveals itself in the "accidents" of contrasting development.

Thus, in common, I think, with the vast majority of my fellow historians, I should like to defend the historically based diversity not only of my own profession but of the different social sciences as well. When sociologists or psychologists argue the necessity of establishing some general social theory, they are tempted to forget the advantages deriving from the varied historical origins of their own disciplines. Psychoanalytic theory—to take this familiar example for one last time—grew up in conjunction with the practice of medicine, and this clinical derivation has heavily influenced its whole development. Similarly the contrasting origins of sociology and anthropology seem largely responsible for the continued separation of two disciplines that work on almost identical subject matter. The founding fathers of sociology were either social reformers or academic theoreticians; the characteristic early anthropologist was a gentleman scholar with a touch of both the poet and the adventurer. If the present-day theoretical sociologists should try to force anthropology into a rigidly mathematical mold, they would squeeze out of it that very quality of intuitive suggestion and imprecision that has made it so congenial to the historical mind and so fruitful in its implications.

There is, then, it seems to me, an irreducible difference in approach between the historians and the model-builders. And any attempt to reconcile the two must take full account of this radical diversity. We shall make no progress toward finding a common ground until we are quite clear in our minds as to the points that cannot be compromised.

To a historian all intellectual "systems" are open. To a mathematically minded social scientist no model is really convincing until it is satisfactorily "closed." He puts all the "parameters" of his problem in terms of precise quantities to the very end that they will tie together and arrive at a neat and elegant sum. He taps "the great resources of modern theoretical statistics as an aid in empirical investigation."[19] The historian, on the other hand, distrusts such precision. Indeed, even the more social science-minded of them—the minority who consent to deal in "systems" at all—think of these systems, as I have already suggested, in Weber's fashion as complementary chains of reasoning whose sum by no means exhausts the explanatory possibilities inherent in the situation at hand.

Similarly, as we have also seen, the pluralistic view of the social universe radically limits the historian's tolerance for anything approaching a definition of the "laws" of social organization. I think it is significant that the only recent attempt at such definition to win even qualified acceptance among historians is one that emphasizes the "abstractive," that is, the noninclusive, character of these laws and that limits them to purely "functional relations." Any effort to arrive at a "global" or "holistic" law and to chart a direction of historical change is dismissed by this writer and by

---

[19] Kenneth J. Arrow, "Mathematical Models in the Social Sciences," *The Policy Sciences,* ed. Lerner and Lasswell, 132.

nearly all analytic philosophers of history as an intellectual will-o'-the-wisp.[20]

Now I am not sure whether the efforts of the model-builders, if directed toward history, would eventuate in all or any of these things, but I think that something of the sort is implied in their confidence that the human mind can quantify and thereby solve virtually all intellectual problems. This confidence, as I shall try to demonstrate shortly, is by no means merely feckless. And it can act as a bracing tonic to the skepticism of the historian, bowed as he is by the weight of centuries of failure to reach any conclusive explanations. At the same time the historian's characteristic skepticism is both his weakness and his strength. To ask him to abandon it would be to call for a betrayal of his deepest philosophical convictions.

The characteristic metaphysic of the contemporary historian is what I should call a "radical nominalism." Once weaned from the comforting abstractions of German idealism, he has settled into the conviction that it is only in the particular and the immediately verifiable that ultimate "reality" lies. This nominalist position was always implicit in one aspect of idealist thinking—in the emphasis that Ranke and his pupils put on individual phenomena and in their insistence on precise research methods. In contrast, the mathematical model-builders, whose philosophical pedigree descends from positivism, look like starry-eyed Platonists. *They* have shifted the emphasis away from the nominalist features of their own tradition (among mathematically oriented economists, for example, one finds a certain condescension for mere "fact-gatherers"). And in its place they have put a faith in the overarching constructions

---

[20] Maurice Mandelbaum, "Societal Laws," *The British Journal for the Philosophy of Science,* VIII (No. 31, 1957), 217–22.

of the human mind that is almost religious in its intensity.

To a historian these constructions are no more than creations of the individual imagination. He ascribes to them no ultimate reality. They are explanatory short cuts, heuristic devices—nothing more. Now the model-builder may object at this point that the same is true of him, that I have been caricaturing his intellectual attitude in order to present too neat a contrast. And in terms of his point of departure he may be perfectly justified in objecting. Initially, no doubt, the model-builder sets forth on his intellectual quest in a frame of mind that is very nearly as skeptical as that of the historian. At the start he may think that he is attempting no more than to establish a tentative scheme of explanation. But as his labors continue, as he comes to have a kind of emotional vested interest in the product of his own mind, this construction begins to take on a "reality" of its own. Its architect finds himself believing in it in a fashion that is far more definite than what empirical procedure would ordinarily countenance.

The same thing, of course, can happen to the historian, and there are many eminent examples from the past to suggest how this can come about. But in contrast to the social scientist, the historian is armed against the temptations of intellectual certainty by an almost congenital self-doubt. To the historical scholar, the greater part of the social universe is a mystery, and he suspects that it will remain so for a long time to come. Indeed, he is quite content to see the realm of certainty limited to the well-defined spheres in which he feels that he can operate with a certain confidence. To the mathematically oriented social scientist, such uncertainty is intolerable: the unknown, the inexplicable, torment him, and he seeks some sort of solution at all costs. In this second sense, then, it is the historian who is the more religiously minded. It is he who advances more hesitantly into the realm of mystery. In this final regard, the original mystical-contemplative spirit of German idealism is with us yet.

So much for our metaphysical parenthesis. If in our implicit philosophy we historians remain back with Weber, or even with the more vaporous Ranke, it does not mean that all traffic with the exact and the quantitative remains closed to us. Quite the contrary. The sphere of quantification is, I think, the first of two areas of investigation in which historical study has already been pushed ahead by contact with the social sciences and in which a great spurt of further progress is in sight.

For at least a generation historians have been applying quantitative methods on a scale previously unimaginable. Statistical applications have revolutionized the study of economic history, more particularly in England, where theoretical competence in economics is allied more closely with historical scholarship than is the case in any other country. The British have also taken the lead in the exploitation of statistical methods for the study of political history. Ever since the publication thirty years ago of Sir Lewis Namier's influential work *The Structure of Politics at the Accession of George III,* a whole school of younger historians, in this country as well as in England, have been dredging away at the material that Namier's book opened up. Biographies, economic affiliations, and voting records have been tabulated and cross-referenced to give a new precision and concreteness to the study of parliamentary bodies and similar elite groups. No longer are we thrown back on vague generalities when we try to write of a political or governing class: for many countries during significant segments of their histories it is now possible to delineate with accuracy just who the members of this class were.

These, however, are simply the initial steps in a perspective of quantification that is beginning to stretch out to infinity. For parliamentary history, or for the more established varieties of economic history that deal in price and income series, statistical applications follow a fairly conventional course. It is quite otherwise with the areas of human experience where historians earlier dismissed the quantitative approach as out of the question. Attitudes, mass sentiments, shifts in popular allegiance—such "qualitative" aspects of life once seemed condemned to a merely impressionistic treatment. Here the "intuitive" generalization or the apt quotation from some contemporary observer had to suffice. It was only when the sociologists and the social psychologists began experimenting with novel techniques for dealing with such matters in the contemporary world that historians were able to see how much had been missed in the standard literary treatments of the past.

Opinion surveys, sampling techniques, projective tests, content analysis, "scaling" and the like are the new procedures with which the scientists of human behavior have enriched our knowledge of contemporary society and, by extrapolation, our understanding of history itself. For it is only half correct to object that these techniques cannot be applied to people who are long since in their graves. Obviously it is impossible to put questions or to administer a projective test to the dead. But one can learn from the results of present-day samplings to look with new eyes at the records of comparable events in the past. Such large-scale movements as revolutions and wars clearly show certain abiding characteristics, and historians have had long experience in applying to them the essential correctives that take account of differences in time and cultural circumstance. A rigorously conducted measurement of attitudes in contemporary society has a direct historical relevance: it can illuminate the past through the new types of interpretation that it suggests.

Here once again the historian may be in no position to make a complete or mechanical application of a novel technique. But his mind will be informed by this technique —he will now be on the lookout for things that earlier would have passed him by. Thus he will be less inclined to think in terms of dichotomies, a Hegelian legacy, and more ready to deal in gradations and continua. And these gradations he will try so far as possible to quantify. He will have learned that the familiar use of adjectives in historical prose often already carries with it a crude kind of quantification. Hence he will be more prepared to substitute numerical ratings for words like "larger" or "smaller"; he will have realized that such ratings, no matter how tentative, will permit him to fit the historical phenomenon in question into a relationship of clear comparability with other phenomena and thus to enlarge his explanatory range. I doubt whether historical study will ever become primarily or even very heavily quantitative in nature. But I am convinced that some of the most significant advances of the next few decades will occur in this sphere.

The second area of fruitful contact between history and social science cannot be specified in quite such concrete terms. For this second type of progress that I envisage is a matter of synthesis rather than of analytical method. It has to do with bringing together the socio-economic and the psychological dimensions in historical explanation.

Again and again in the earlier part of this essay I have

referred to the methodological writings of Max Weber. I have done so, of course, because I believe that they state in a classic fashion that is still valid today the basic elements of the relation between history and social science. They have, however, one glaring weakness. Weber was almost totally ignorant of the psychological theory of his day, more particularly of the work of Freud, and when he traced his complementary chains of economic and spiritual causation, he was unable to enrich the latter with interpretations drawn from psychoanalytic observation. In his writings the socio-economic dimension alone was clearly defined; the spiritual aspect remained in the realm of mystery.

Since Weber's day a number of social theorists, strongly influenced by the psychoanalytic approach, have tried to define the emotional and "spiritual" attitudes of large numbers of people in specified historical stages of the societies to which they have belonged. Thus David Riesman has traced three successive "directions" in which the dominant ethos within American society has manifested itself; Theodor Adorno has outlined the configurations of an "authoritarian personality" in a contemporary setting; Erich Fromm has contrasted the relative emotional security that nineteenth-century society provided with the terrors and frustrations that have prompted a twentieth-century "escape from freedom." All of these interpretations have been impressionistic. All have carried a heavy freight of personal emotion. Yet their sum has suggested the possibilities of a new type of social theory that combines clinical diagnosis of individual problems with a bold typology of the sentiments of the mass.

Now the notion of successive stages in the history of societies is a very old one in political and economic speculation. We may think of Marx's threefold evolution from feudalism through capitalism to socialism and of Tönnies' *Gemeinschaft-Gesellschaft* sequence, dear to three generations of German thinkers. More recently economic historians and sociologists have begun to refine on the standard German vocabulary: they have substituted some such term as "traditional" society for what Marx called feudalism and they have narrowed the definition of eighteenth- and nineteenth-century capitalism by identifying it with specifically "bourgeois" practices. To these two stages they have added a third phase of "industrial" society, that is, a configuration of phenomena uniquely characteristic of contemporary urban conditions.[21] This third stage they have viewed as either capitalist or socialist: the older distinctions have become less important, as interest has shifted away from the question of technical property rights and has focused on such manifestations—common to both types of ownership in a highly industrialized society—as bureaucratization, a consumer-oriented economy and the growth of a white-collar class.

A natural extension of this threefold typology of socio-economic change would be to equate the third or "industrial" stage with the aspects of mass psychology that writers like Riesman, Fromm and Adorno have found characteristic of the contemporary scene. I do not know whether anyone has yet made such an equation explicit. But it hovers in the background of much of the social speculation that is going on at the present time. In "informing" so much of our contemporary thinking, it suggests one of the major approaches that lie before us in seeking to combine socio-economic analysis with psychological understanding.

---

[21] See, for example, John E. Sawyer, "Strains in the Social Structure of Modern France," *Modern France: Problems of the Third and Fourth Republics,* ed. Edward Mead Earle (Princeton, 1951), 293–312.

Another approach, still more generalized in character, has already been suggested by the references I have made to the congeniality of cultural anthropology with the mind of the historian. The anthropologist has always dealt with a cultural totality. From the start his aim has been similar to the one at which the more imaginative historians of today have just arrived—that is, to grasp in a coherent pattern the economic, social and psychological manifestations of a given society. For a long time the anthropologist has been trying to define "the fundamental and distinctive cultural configurations that pattern existence and condition the thoughts and emotions of the individuals who participate in those cultures." [22] Hence he has seen rather more sharply than has the historical scholar both the possibilities and the pitfalls of this approach. At the present time it is primarily from anthropology that the would-be practitioners of the newer type of history can learn how to go about their unfamiliar tasks.

More concretely this means some experimenting with the techniques of field investigation. A generation ago Marc Bloch's epoch-making studies of French rural history showed how much the past could be illuminated by on-the-spot observation of contemporary practices.[23] The implication of Bloch's work was a new kind of historical technique that would systematically extrapolate from present-day vestiges of earlier conditions—that would undertake a reconstruction of vanished practices on the basis of the traces of them that could still be directly observed. This sort of learning from traditions, from linguistic usage, from architectural and technological remains, was, of course, Vico's

---

[22] Ruth Benedict, *Patterns of Culture* (Boston, 1934), 55.
[23] More particularly in *Les caractères originaux de l'histoire rurale française* (Oslo, 1931).

unparalleled contribution to historical study. A century later it was brought to general attention and applied on a large scale by Michelet. But I think it was Bloch who first systematized the new approach for the uses of the ordinary historical scholar.

Obviously such field work, as Bloch well knew, could yield better results in the countryside than in the city. In great urban agglomerations the traces of the past are almost obliterated; in rural areas a trained and alert observer can frequently find them intact. Thus the application to Western societies of anthropological field techniques originally devised for preliterate cultures has worked best in small, rural communities. It is here that it has proved possible to discover not only the living past but a way of life whose salient features are still understood and explicitly recognized. In short, an on-the-spot study of a small community seems to me the best possible training ground for the historian whose mind is oriented toward social and psychological synthesis. And there is a model for such study in Laurence Wylie's sympathetic account of a village in southern France[24]—the work of a humanist coming only late in his career to social science method.

But it is far more than mere technical training that the young historian can derive from the experience of community study. More important than that, he can begin to learn how the group mind works, how individual reactions conform to established patterns. From observation of a microcosm of a wider society, he can gain firsthand experience that he can subsequently apply to larger social units both of the present time and of the past. In a small, readily comprehensible framework, he can grasp the nature

---

[24] Laurence Wylie, *Village in the Vaucluse* (Cambridge, Mass., 1957).

of the thought and emotion that express themselves in standardized practices; he can learn to recognize the patterns of speech and action that embody a symbolic way of thinking. In most general terms, he can begin to grope his way toward the definition of the central, grouping symbols that in their infinite variety give meaning to human life in established societies both large and small.

To use the words "central, grouping symbols" is already to give the alarm to the methodologically timid. For it sounds like trying to define some "spirit of the times"—that cultural Lorelei that has seduced generation after generation of speculative historians. Or, still worse, it seems to be an expression of sympathy with Spengler and his ilk in seeking one or two prime symbols that will stand for whole civilizations. By my injunction to set forth in search of central symbolic configurations I have apparently thrown the gates wide open to the wildest sort of historical speculation.

Now such an accusation is not totally unjustified. As I shall try to show in a moment, I think that a frankly speculative treatment has a place in historical method that has not always been sufficiently recognized. And this, like the whole notion of defining symbols, has an irremediable vagueness about it. Indeed, these are precisely the points where the whole element of art and literature enters into historical explanation—an element, as I have suggested, that history more particularly shares with cultural anthropology among the social sciences. At one point or another history necessarily passes over from science into art: the main thing is to be sure that this point of passage has been well chosen.

I mentioned at the start of this essay the tendency of historical writing to oscillate between highly abstract and excessively detailed planes of interpretation. And I offered it as one of my purposes to seek a middle level. What I have said earlier about "schematization" and the application of social science method to historical study has obviously constituted one approach to this middle ground. And what I have just now been saying about "central symbols" offers another such approach. For in this peculiarly "artistic" aspect of historical interpretation, a middle level is similarly aimed at, but it is a middle term of a less easily recognizable kind. Its characteristic imprecision obscures the things that distinguish it from what is vastly general on the one hand and what is merely individual on the other.

The sort of symbolic understanding of society that I have proposed does not undertake to subsume whole civilizations in Spenglerian fashion under a few key terms (although it may well be enriched and "informed" by Spengler's heroic effort at cultural synthesis). Nor, at the other end of the scale, does it try to delineate in artistic fashion what is highly individual and hence "picturesque." It seeks, rather, for something that is far more delimited and tangible than the former and far more generalized than the latter. It deals with real societies, real, that is, in the sense that their members actually feel themselves to belong to such communities and in the sense that some part of them can be observed and even lived in by the historian today. These societies are not brilliant devices of the historian's imagination like Spengler's much-disputed "Magian" civilization: they are smaller and more precisely defined, running all the way from the sort of village that Wylie studied to the national communities that literary figures like Leonardo Olschki and Rebecca West have tried to assess.[25] And the symbols that seem to characterize them are simi-

---

[25] Leonardo Olschki, *The Genius of Italy* (New York, 1949); Rebecca West, *Black Lamb and Grey Falcon* (New York, 1941).

larly tangible: far from being the product of mere excogitations of the study, they are derived from social and psychological observation and from practical linguistic experience.

But still an irreducible imprecision remains. And for this the social scientist or the more scientifically minded type of historian is inclined to apologize. In social scientists (anthropologists excepted) such an attitude is pardonable. Their whole professional ethos is bound up with the notion of rigor and "testability." In historians, however, it is less understandable. As I have noted again and again, the very imprecision of the historian's traditional approach has been both his fatal weakness and his most precious source of strength.

And so the point has at last arrived to shift over to the offensive. Throughout the bulk of this essay I have cast the historian in a comparatively humble role—as a learner sitting at the feet of his colleagues in the social sciences. I have tried to take full account of the varied range of social science method and approach from which the historian can profit. At the same time I have attempted to mark the points at which the historian must refuse to modify his definition of his own calling. Now the time has come to let the historian speak out. I should like to conclude this essay by turning the subject around and suggesting one or two respects in which the social scientist may profit by the historian's example.

I spoke a moment back of the virtues of speculation. It is here, I think, that contemporary social science, more particularly in the United States, is failing to do its job. Since Karl Mannheim and Joseph Schumpeter passed from the scene, there has been almost no one both willing and qualified to take a total view of social change in our time in its broadest historical setting. The great tradition of wide-ranging historical and economic sociology has just about expired: it had its origin in Germany with Marx, and it was there that the Nazis killed it off by perverting its practitioners (like Sombart) or driving them off into culturally alien lands in which they could find few like-minded pupils. At the present time neither economics nor sociology is fulfilling this function. The chair of speculative social thought stands vacant. And in the absence of other claimants it is the historians who are beginning to move in.

And why not? If social scientists of one sort or another do not deal with the major questions of our time, then someone else will, and the public will lap up his work. If those who have been systematically trained for the task evade it, then the less qualified—the journalists and the purveyors of sensationalism—will take the matter into their own hands. The more imaginative historians know this, and they are quite prepared to assume the new responsibility and the burden of professional opprobrium that goes with it.

Such are the perils of dealing with historical problems of real magnitude. For it is only in rare instances that the sort of "middle-level" generalization that I have been advocating can attain any true scientific rigor. Most of the time the schematizations that the historian may devise satisfy only very partially the usual canons of scientific method. The evidence is too slim. The bridges thrown between one cluster of data and another are too shaky. The resulting hypotheses display only a partial internal consistency: they are full of unresolved contradictions. So much for the sins of speculative method; they are so apparent and so many that we need enumerate them no further.

Yet in my own teaching and writing I have found that it is precisely here that the contemporary historian makes his chief contribution. Very early in the course of seminar instruction, I observed that the most interesting and important things that the students had to say were those which they could footnote least adequately. The really original parts of their papers dealt in alternatives and might-have-beens and all sorts of other historical possibilities of doubtful pedigree. Similarly in my own more informal efforts to explain contemporary history I have found that the vital and central problems are the ones that are beset with the most perplexing difficulties. The analysis of fascist systems, for instance, simply does not lend itself to rigorous comparative treatment: the number of cases is too small (only two full-blown ones), and the available explanations—mostly economic or psychological—are too heterogeneous in character to permit us to dovetail them in any unambiguous fashion. Yet I propose to continue in these comparative speculations and to urge my students to do the same. For I am convinced that it is only in this fashion that we can bring some sort of initial order into the appalling welter of "facts" that contemporary history offers.

An initial order—a first rough approximation at an explanatory scheme—this is the sole and sufficient apologia we may give for historical speculation. Only in this fashion can we make a mass of apparently fragmentary and incoherent data comprehensible to ourselves and hence communicable to others. As all natural scientists know, the building of hypotheses springs originally from imagination and "intuitive" processes too subterranean for the individual to trace. And the same is true of social science. Here the historian is at a particular advantage. His definition of his own calling endows him with a flexibility in this realm that is denied to social scientists in the stricter sense. The historian's tradition of kinship with literature and the arts gives sanction and approval to the free play of his imagination.

History has always thought of itself as an inclusive, a mediating discipline. Once it linked philosophy with poetry. Now it is linking literature with social science. History's new consciousness of its debt to social science need not mean a weakening of its artistic ties. Indeed, the contrary is the case. For it is history that can lead social science itself along the path of imagination and bold hypothesis toward literature—back to the realms in which it dwelt and prospered in the century and three quarters of great achievement that began with Montesquieu and ended with Weber.

History and Theory:

The Concept of Scientific History

Sir Isaiah Berlin

Sir Isaiah Berlin took the degree of M.A. at Oxford, where he was a scholar at Corpus Christi College, graduating in successive years in Literae Humaniores (1931) and Philosophy, Politics and Economics (1932). He was lecturer in philosophy at New College and fellow of All Souls College (1932–1938), fellow of New College (1938–1950) and research fellow of All Souls College (1950–1957). Since 1957 he has been Chichele Professor of Social and Political Philosophy in the University of Oxford.

He lectured and taught at Harvard University in 1949, 1951 and 1953, and returned as visiting professor in 1962. In 1952 he was Mary Flexner Lecturer at Bryn Mawr College, and in 1955 he was Alexander White Visiting Professor at the University of Chicago. He has lectured at many other universities in Britain and on the continent.

He is a Companion of the Order of the British Empire, a Fellow of the British Academy, having served as Vice President of the latter in 1962, and a Fellow of the American Academy of Arts and Sciences.

He is the author of Karl Marx: His Life and Environment; The Hedgehog and the Fox: An Essay on Tolstoy's View of History; Moses Hess and the Marvellous Decade, *studies of political radicals in the nineteenth century; and* The Age of Enlightenment. *He is a frequent contributor to philosophical* and literary journals, and his essays on politics and the philosophy of history include "Historical Inevitability," "Two Concepts of Liberty," "John Stuart Mill and the Ends of Life," and "Political Ideas in the Twentieth Century."

A. History, according to Aristotle, is an account of what individual human beings have done and suffered. More widely still, history is what historians do. Is history, in this sense, a science, as, let us say, physics or biology or psychology are sciences? And if not, should it seek to be one? And if it fails to be one, what prevents it? Is this due to human weakness, or to the nature of the subject, or does the very problem rest on a confusion between the concept of history and that of natural science? These have been questions that have occupied the minds of both philosophers and philosophically minded historians at least since the beginning of the nineteenth century, when men became self-conscious about the purpose and logic of their intellectual activities. But two centuries before that, Descartes had already denied to history any claim to be a serious study. Those who accepted the validity of the Cartesian criterion of what constitutes rational method could (and did) ask how they could find the clear and simple elements of which historical judgments were composed, and into which they could be analyzed; where were the definitions, the logical transformation rules, the rules of inference, the rigorously deduced conclusions? While this confused amalgam of memories and travelers' tales, fables and chroniclers' stories, moral reflections and gossip, might be a harmless pastime, it was beneath the dignity of serious men seeking what alone is worth seeking—the discovery of the truth in accordance with the principles and rules which alone guarantee scientific validity.

Ever since this doctrine of what was and what was not a

science was enunciated, those who have thought about the nature of historical studies have labored under the stigma of the Cartesian condemnation. Some have tried to show that history could be made respectable by being assimilated to one of the natural sciences, whose overwhelming success and prestige in the seventeenth and eighteenth centuries held out promise of rich fruit wherever their methods were applicable; others declared that history was indeed a science, but a science in some different sense, with its own methods and canons, no less exacting than those of the sciences of nature, but resting on foundations different from them; others defiantly declared that history was indeed subjective, impressionistic, incapable of being made rigorous, a branch of literature, or an expression of a personal vision —or that of a class, a church, a nation—a form of self-expression which was, indeed, its pride and justification: it laid no claim to universal objectivity, and preferred to be judged as an art or a philosophy of life, not as a science. Still others have tried to draw distinctions between sociology, which was a true science, and history, which was an art or, perhaps, something altogether *sui generis,* neither a science nor an art, but a discipline with its own structure and purposes, misunderstood by those who tried to draw false analogies between it and other intellectual activities.

B. In any case, the logic of historical thought and the validity of its credentials are issues of comparatively little interest to the leading logicians of our day. The reasons for this are not far to seek. Nevertheless it remains surprising that philosophers pay more attention to the logic of such natural sciences as mathematics and physics, which comparatively few of them know well at first hand, and neglect that of history and the other humane studies, with which in the course of their normal education they tend to be more familiar.

C. Be that as it may, it is not difficult to see why there has been a strong desire to regard history as a science. History purports to deal with facts. The most successful method of identifying, discovering and inferring facts is that of the natural sciences. This is the only region of human experience, at any rate in modern times, in which progress has indubitably been made. It is natural to wish to apply methods successful and authoritative in one sphere to another, where there is far less agreement among specialists. The whole trend of modern empiricism, moreover, has tended towards such a view. History is an account of what men have done and of what has happened to them. Man is largely, some would say wholly, an object in nature: his bodily wants can be studied empirically as those of other animals. Basic human needs for, say, food or shelter or procreation, and his other biological or physiological requirements, do not seem to have altered greatly through the millennia, and the laws of the interplay of these needs with one another and with the human environment can in principle be studied by the methods of the biological and, perhaps, the psychological sciences. This applies particularly to the unintended results of man's collective activities which play so large a part in influencing his life, and which can be explained in purely causal terms as fields of force or functional correlations of human action and other natural processes. This bears the plain marks of the subject-matter of a natural science. If only we could find a series of natural laws connecting at one end, the biological and physiological states and processes of human beings, with, at the other, the equally observable patterns of their conduct—their social activities in the wider sense—and so establish a coherent system of regularities deducible from a comparatively small number of general laws (as Newton had so triumphantly done in physics), we should have in our hands a science of human behavior. Then we could perhaps afford to ignore as secondary such intermediate phenomena as human feelings, thoughts, volitions, of which men's lives seem to themselves to be largely composed, but which do not lend themselves easily to exact measurement. If these data could be regarded as by-products of other, scientifically observable and measurable, processes, then we could predict the publicly observable behavior of men (what more can a science ask for?) without taking the vaguer and more elusive data of introspection into much account. This would be the scientific sociology dreamed of by the materialists of the French Enlightenment, particularly Condillac and Condorcet and their nineteenth-century followers—Comte, Buckle, Spencer, Taine and many a modern behaviorist, positivist and "physicalist" since their day.

D. What kind of science would history constitute? The traditional division of the sciences is into the inductive and the deductive. Unless one claimed acquaintance with *a priori* propositions or rules, derived not from observation, but from knowledge, based on intuition or revelation, of the laws governing the behavior of men and of their goals, or of the specific purposes of their creator—and few historians since the Middle Ages have openly professed to possess such knowledge—this science could not be wholly deductive. But is it then inductive? It is difficult or impossible to conduct large-scale experiments on human beings, and knowledge must therefore largely rest on observation. However, this disability has not prevented astronomy or geology from becoming flourishing sciences, and the mechanists of the eighteenth century confidently looked forward to a time when the application of the methods of the mathematical sciences to human affairs would explode all myths, such as those of the inner light, a personal deity, an immaterial soul, freedom of the will, and so forth; and so solve all social problems by means of a scientific sociology as clear, exact and capable of predicting future behavior as, to use Condorcet's phrase, the sciences that study the societies of bees or beavers. In the nineteenth century this claim was thought at once too trivial and too extravagant. It became clear that the methods and concepts of the mechanists were not capable of accounting for growth and change; and the adoption of the more complex vitalistic or evolutionary categories and models served to demarcate the procedures of the biological from those of the physical sciences; the former were clearly more appropriate to the growth and development of human beings. In the twentieth century psychology has begun to assume the role that biology had played in the previous century, and its methods and discoveries with regard both to individuals and to groups have in their turn transformed our approach to history.

E. Why had history so long to wait to become a science? Buckle, perhaps the most passionate believer in the science of history who ever lived, explained this very simply by the fact that historians were "inferior in mental power" to the mathematicians and physicists and chemists. He declared that those sciences advanced fastest which in the first instance attracted the attention of the cleverest men, and their successes naturally in their turn attracted other able heads into their services. In other words, if men as gifted as Galileo or Newton, or even Laplace or Faraday, had devoted themselves to dealing with the disordered mass of truth and falsehood that went by the name of history, they could soon have set it to rights and made a firmly built, clear, and fertile natural science of it.[1] This was a promise

---

[1] "In regard to nature, events apparently the most irregular and capricious have been explained and have been shown to be in accord-

held out by those who were, very understandably, hypnotized by the magnificent progress of the natural sciences of their day. Intelligent and skeptical thinkers like Taine and Renan in France, not to speak of really passionate positivists like Comte, and, in most of his writings, Marx, profoundly believed in this prospect. Their hopes have scarcely been fulfilled. It may be profitable to ask why this is so.

F. Before an answer to this question is attempted, two further sources of the belief that history can, at least in principle, be transformed into a natural science may be noted. The first is perhaps conveyed best by the metaphors that, at any rate since the nineteenth century, all educated men

---

ance with certain fixed and universal laws. This has been done because men of ability, and above all, men of patient, untiring thought, have studied natural events with the view of discovering their regularity: and if human events were subjected to a similar treatment, we have every right to expect similar results. . . . Whoever is at all acquainted with what has been done during the last two centuries, must be aware that every generation demonstrates some events to be regular and predictable, which the preceding generation had declared to be irregular and unpredictable: so that the marked tendency of advancing civilization is to strengthen our belief in the universality of order, of method, and of law. This being the case, it follows that if any facts, or class of facts, have not yet been reduced to order, we, so far from pronouncing them to be irreducible, should rather be guided by our experience of the past, and should admit the probability that what we now call inexplicable will at some future time be explained. The expectation of discovering regularity in the midst of confusion is so familiar to scientific men, that among the most eminent of them it becomes an article of faith; and if the same expectation is not generally found among historians, it must be ascribed partly to their being of inferior ability to the investigators of nature, and partly to the greater complexity of those social phenomena with which their studies are concerned. . . . The most celebrated historians are manifestly inferior to the most successful cultivators of physical science: no one having devoted himself to history who in point of intellect is at all to be compared with Kepler, Newton, or many others . . . [nevertheless] I entertain little doubt that before another century has elapsed, the chain of evidence will be complete, and it will be as rare to find an historian who denies the undeviating regularity of the moral world, as it now is to find a philosopher who denies the regularity of the material world." Henry Thomas Buckle, *History of Civilization in England*, Vol. I, Ch. I.

tend to use. When we speak of rational as opposed to utopian policies, we tend to say of the latter that they ignore, or are "defeated" by, the "inexorable logic of the (historical) facts" or "the wheels of history" which it is idle to try to stay. We speak of the futility of defying "the forces of history," or the absurdity of efforts to "put the clock back" or "to restore the past." We speak of the youth, the maturity, the decay of peoples or cultures, of the ebb and flow of social movements, of the rise and fall of nations. Such language conveys the idea of an inexorably fixed time order—"the river of time" on which we float, and which we must willy-nilly accept; a moving stair which we have not created, but on which we are borne, as if it obeyed some natural law governing the order and shape of events—in this case, events consisting of, or at any rate affecting, human lives, activities, and experiences. Metaphorical and misleading though such uses of words may be, they are pointers to categories and concepts in terms of which we conceive the "stream of history" as something possessing a certain objective pattern that we ignore at our peril. It is a short step from this to conclude that whatever has a pattern, exhibits regularities capable of being condensed in laws; and the systematic interconnection of laws is the content of a natural science.

The second source is deeper still. Patterns of growth, or of the march of events, can plausibly be represented as a succession of causes and effects, capable of being systematized by natural science. But sometimes we speak as if something more fundamental than mere empirical connections (which Idealist philosophers call "mechanical," "external" or "brute conjunctions") give their unity to the aspects or the successive phases, of the existence of the human race on earth. When we say, for instance, that it is absurd to blame Richelieu for not acting like Bismarck because it is obvious that Richelieu could not have acted like a man living in Germany in the nineteenth century; and that conversely Bismarck could not have done what Richelieu accomplished, because the seventeenth century had its own character, very different from the deeds, events, characteristics of the eighteenth century which it uniquely determined, and which in their turn uniquely determined those of the nineteenth; what we are then affirming is that this order is an objective order; that those who do not understand that what is possible in one age may be wholly inconceivable in another, fail to understand something universal and fundamental about the only way in which social life, or the human mind, or economic growth, or some other sequence, not merely does, but can, or perhaps must, develop. Similarly, when we say that the proposition that *Hamlet* was written at the court of Genghis Khan in Outer Mongolia is not merely false but absurd; that if someone seriously supposes that it could have been written at that time and in that place, he is not merely ignorant or in error, but out of his mind; that *Hamlet* not merely was not, but could not have been, written there or then—in short, that we can dismiss this hypothesis without discussion—what is it that entitles us to feel so certain? What kind of "could not" is this "could not"? We do not rule out propositions asserting possibilities of this kind as being grotesquely false on scientific, that is, empirical-inductive grounds. We call them grotesque because they conflict with presuppositions which govern our whole thinking about the world—the categories in terms of which alone we conceive such basic notions as man, society, history, development, growth, barbarism, civilization and the like. These presuppositions may turn out to be false or misleading (as, for example, teleology or deism are considered to have been by positivists or atheists), but they are not refuted by experiment or empirical observation. They are destroyed or transformed by those changes in the total outlook of a man or a milieu or a culture which it is the hardest (and the most important) test of the histories of ideas (and, in the end, of history as such) to be able to explain. What is here involved is a deeply ingrained, widespread, long-lived *Weltanschauung*—the unquestioning (and not necessarily valid) assumption of one particular objective order of events or facts. Sometimes it is a vertical order—succession in time—which makes us realize that the events or institutions of, say, the fourteenth century, because they were what they were, of necessity (however we analyze this sort of necessity), and not just as a matter of fact—contingently—occurred earlier than those of the sixteenth, which were "shaped," that is, in some sense, determined (some would say, caused) by them; so that anyone who tries to date the works of Shakespeare before those of Dante, or to omit the fifteenth century altogether, fitting the end of the fourteenth into the beginning of the sixteenth century without a break, can be convicted of suffering from a defect different in kind—not degree—from, and one far worse than, ignorance or lack of scientific method. At other times we conceive of the order as "horizontal"; that is, it underlies the perception of the interconnections between different aspects of the same stage of culture—the kinds of assumptions and categories that the antimechanistic German philosophers of culture, Herder and his disciples (and before them, Vico), brought to light. It is this—the historical—sense that is said to enable us to perceive that a certain type of legal structure is "intimately connected" with an economic activity, or moral outlook, or style of writing or of dancing or of worship; it is by means of this gift (whatever may be its nature) that we recognize various manifestations of the human spirit as "belonging to" this or that culture or nation or historical period, although these manifestations may be as different from one another as the way in which men form letters on paper are from their system of land tenure. Without this faculty we should attach no sense to such notions as the typical, or the normal, or the discordant, or the anachronistic, and consequently we should be unable to conceive the history of an institution as an intelligible pattern, or attribute a work of art to its time and civilization and milieu, or indeed be able to understand or explain how one phase of a civilization "generates" or "determines" another. This sense of what remains identical or unitary in differences and in change (of which Idealist philosophers have made altogether too much) is also a dominant factor in giving us the sense of unalterable trends, of the "one-directional" flow of history. From this it is easy to pass to the far more questionable belief that whatever is unalterable is so only because it obeys laws, and whatever obeys laws can always be systematized into a science.

G. These are among the many factors that have made men crave for a natural science of history. All seemed ready, particularly in the nineteenth century, for the formulation of this new, powerful and illuminating discipline, which would do away with the chaotic accumulation of facts, conjectures and rules of thumb that had been treated with such disdain by Descartes and his scientifically-minded successors. All was ready, but virtually nothing came forth. No general laws were formulated—nor even moderately reliable maxims—from which historians could deduce (together with knowledge of the initial conditions) either what would happen next, or what had happened in the past. The great machine which was to rescue them from the tedious labors of adding fact to fact and of attempting to construct a coherent account out of their handpicked material, remained no more than a plan in the head of a cracked inventor. The immense labor-saving invention which would itself order the facts, deduce the right conclusions, and offer the proper explanations, removing the need for the uncertain, old-fashioned, hand-operated tools with which historians had fumbled their way in the unregenerate past, remained a bogus prospectus, a curiosity of an extravagant imagination, like the perpetual motion machine. Neither psychologists nor sociologists, neither the ambitious Comte nor the more modest Wundt, had been able to create the new instrument: the "nomothetic" sciences—the system of laws and rules under which the factual material could be grouped so as to yield new knowledge—remained stillborn.

One of the criteria of a natural science is rightly regarded as being its capacity for prediction; or, in the case of an historical study, retrodiction—filling in gaps in the past for which no direct testimony exists by extrapolation in accordance with the relevant rules or laws. A method of this conjectural sort is employed in archeology or paleontology where vast gaps in knowledge exist and there is no better—more dependable—avenue to factual truth in the absence of concrete factual evidence. In archeology we make efforts to link our knowledge of one remote period to our knowledge of another by trying to reconstruct what must, or at least may have, occurred to account for the transition from one stage to the other through many unknown intermediate phases. But this way of filling gaps is rightly regarded as a none too reliable method of discovery of the past, and one to which no one would wish to resort if he could find the more concrete kind of evidence on which we base our knowledge of the historical—as opposed to prehistoric—period of human life; still less as a "scientific" substitute for it.

H. What would such a science look like, supposing that one were able to formulate it? It would, presumably, consist of causal or functional correlations—a system of interrelated general propositions of the type "whenever or wherever x then or there y"—variables into which precise dates and places could be fitted; it would possess two forms: the "pure" and the applied. The "pure" sciences of social statics or social dynamics, as Herbert Spencer too optimistically called sociology, would then be related to the applied science of history, somewhat as the pure science of physics is related to the science of mechanics, or at least as anatomy applies to the diagnosis of specific cases by a physician. If it existed, such a science would have revolutionized the old empirical, hand-woven history by mechanizing it, as astronomy abolished the rules of thumb accumulated by Babylonian stargazers, or as Newtonian physics transformed older cosmologies. No such science exists. Before we ask why this is so, it would perhaps be profitable to consider some of the more obvious ways in which history, as it is written, differs from a natural science conceived in this fashion.

I. Let me begin by one conspicuous difference between history and the natural sciences. Whereas in a developed natural science we consider it more rational to put our confidence in general propositions or laws than in specific phenomena (indeed this is part of the definition of rationality), this rule does not seem to operate successfully in history. Let me give the simplest possible type of example. One of the common-sense generalizations that we regard as most firmly established is that the normal inhabitants of this planet can see the sun rise every morning. Supposing a man were to say that on a given morning he had not, despite repeated attempts, seen the sun rise; and that since one negative instance is, by the rules of our ordinary logic, sufficient to kill a general proposition, he regarded his carefully carried out observation as fatal not merely to the hitherto accepted generalization about the succession of night and day, but to the entire system of celestial mechanics and, indeed, of physics, which purports to reveal the causes of this phenomenon. This startling claim would not normally be regarded as a conclusion to be unhesitatingly accepted. Our first reaction would be to try to construct an *ad hoc* hypothesis to save our system of physics, supported as it is by the most systematic accumulation of controlled observation and deductive reasoning made by men. We should suggest to the objector that perhaps he was not looking at the right portion of the sky; that clouds intervened; that he was distracted; that his eyes were closed; that he was asleep; that he was suffering from an hallucination; that he was using words in unfamiliar senses; that he was lying or insane; we should advance other explanations, any one of which would be compatible with his statement, and yet preserve physical science intact. It would not be rational to jump to the immediate conclusion that if the man, in our considered judgment, had told the truth, the whole of our hard-won physics must be rejected, or even modified. No doubt, if the phenomenon repeated itself, and other men failed to perceive the sun rise under normal conditions, some physical hypotheses, or indeed laws, might have to be drastically altered, or even rejected; perhaps the foundations of our physical sciences would have to be built anew. But we should only embark on this in the last resort. Yet if an historian were to attempt to cast doubt on—or explain away—some piece of individual observation of a type not otherwise suspect, say, that Napoleon had been seen in a three-cornered hat at a given moment during the battle of Austerlitz; and if the historian did so solely because he put his faith, for whatever reason, in a theory or law according to which French generals or heads of state never wore three-cornered hats during battles, his method, one can safely assert, would not meet with universal or immediate recognition from his profession. Any procedure designed to discredit the testimony of normally reliable witnesses or documents as, let us say, lies or forgeries, or as being defective at the very point at which the report about Napoleon's hat occurred, would be liable to be regarded as itself suspect, as an attempt to alter the facts to fit a theory. I have chosen a crude and trivial instance; it would not be difficult to think of more sophisticated examples, where an historians lays himself open to the charge of trying to press the facts into the service of a particular theory. Such historians are accused of being prisoners of their theories; they are accused of being fanatical or cranky or doctrinaire, of misrepresenting, or misreading reality to fit in with their obsessions, and the like. Addiction to theory—being doctrinaire—is a term of abuse when applied to historians; yet it is not an insult if applied to a natural scientist. We are saying nothing derogatory if we say of a natural scientist that he is in the grip of a theory. We may complain if we think that his theory is false, but we do not deplore the fact that he is trying to fit the facts into the pattern of a theory; for it is his business to be a theorist. It is the business of a natural scientist to formulate doctrines—true rather than false, but, above all, doctrines; for natural science is nothing if it is not a systematic interlacing of theories and doctrines, built up inductively, or by hypothetical deductive methods, or whatever other method is considered best (logically reputable, rational, fruitful) by the most competent practitioners in the field. It seems clear that whereas in history we more often than not attach greater credence to particular facts than to general propositions, however well supported, from which these facts could in theory be deduced, in a natural science the opposite seems to be the case: there it is more rational to place credence in a properly supported general theory—say, that of gravitation—than in specific facts. This difference alone, whatever its root, must cast sharp doubt upon any attempt to draw an analogy between the methods of history and those of natural science.

J. It may be objected at this point that the only logical justification for belief in particular facts must involve general propositions, and therefore always in the end rests on induction. For what other way of justifying beliefs about facts have we? The first of these assertions is true, but the second is not, and their conflation leads to confusion. It needs no deep reflection to realize that all our thought is shot through with general propositions. All thinking involves classification; all classification involves general terms. My very notion of Napoleon or hats or battles, involves some general beliefs about the entities which these words denote. Moreover, my reasons for trusting an eye-witness account or a document entail judgments about the reliability of different kinds of testimony, or the range within which the behavior of individuals is or is not variable and the like—judgments which are certainly general. But (a) it is a far cry from the scattered generalizations implicit in the everyday use of words (or ideas) to the systematic structure of even the most rudimentary science;[2] (b) I am

---

[2] This can be put in another way by saying that the generalizations of history, like those of ordinary thought, are largely unconnected; so that a change in the degree of belief of any one of these does not, as in a natural science, automatically affect the status of all the others. This is a crucial difference.

certain, for example, that I am not at this moment the Emperor of Mars dreaming a dream in which I am a university teacher on the earth; but I should be exceedingly hard put to it to justify my certainty by inductive methods that avoid circularity. Most of the certainties on which our lives are founded would scarcely pass this test. The vast majority of the types of reasoning on which our beliefs rest, or by which we should seek to justify them if they were challenged, are not reducible to formal deductive or inductive schemata, or combinations of them. If I am asked what rational grounds I have for supposing that I am not on Mars, or that the Emperor Napoleon existed and was not merely a sun myth, and if in answer to this I try to make explicit the general propositions which entail this conclusion, together with the specific evidence for them, and the evidence for the reliability of this evidence, and the evidence for that evidence in its turn, I shall not get very far. The web is too complex, the elements too many and not easily isolated and tested one by one, as anyone can satisfy himself by trying to analyze and state them explicitly. The true reason for accepting the propositions that I live on earth, and that an Emperor Napoleon I existed, is that to assert their contradictories is to destroy too much of what we take for granted about the present and the past. Any given generalization may be capable of being tested or refined by inductive or other scientific tests; but we accept the total texture, compounded as it is out of literally countless strands—including both general and particular beliefs—without the possibility—even in principle—of any test for it in its totality. For the total texture is what we begin and end with. There is no Archimedean point outside it whence we can survey the whole of it and pronounce upon it. We can test one part in terms of another, but not the whole, as it were, at one go. When the proposition that the earth was flat was abandoned, this wrought great havoc in the assumptions of common sense; but it could not in principle destroy them all. For in that case nothing would have remained that could be called thinking or criticism. It is the sense of the general texture of experience—the most rudimentary awareness of such patterns—that constitutes knowledge of this noninductive, nondeductive kind. Any one proposition or set of propositions can be shaken in terms of those that remain fixed; and then these latter in their turn; but not all simultaneously. All my beliefs cannot be overthrown. Even if the ground beneath one of my feet is crumbling, my other foot must rest securely planted, at least for the time being; otherwise there is no possibility of thought or communication. It is this network of our most general assumptions, called common-sense knowledge, that historians rightly and inescapably take for granted.

K. Let us pursue this a little further. The natural sciences consist of logically linked laws about the behavior of objects in the world. In certain cases these generalizations can be represented in the form of an ideal model—an imaginary entity, whose characteristics are by definition what they must be if the entity in question obeys the general laws in question, and can be exhaustively described solely in terms of obeying these laws; that is, it consists of nothing but what instantiates such laws. Such models (or deductive schemata) exhibit most vividly and clearly the laws which we attempt to apply to reality; the objects of the natural world can then be described in terms of the degree of deviation that they exhibit from the ideal model. The degree to which these differences can be systematically described, the simplicity of the model, and the range of its application, is one of the criteria of the success or failure of a given science to perform its task. The electron, the gene, the state of perfect competition, the ideal democracy, are all such models; they are useful to the degree to which the actual behavior of real entities in the world can be represented with lesser or greater precision in terms of their deviation from the frictionless behavior of the perfect model. This is the purpose for which the model is constructed; its usefulness corresponds to the degree to which it fulfills it.

Such a model or deductive schema is conspicuously absent in normal historical writing; if only because the general propositions out of which it must be constructed, and which, if they existed, would require to be precisely formulated, turn out to be impossible to specify. General concepts do, of course, occur in history—notions like "community," or "state," or "revolution," or "trend of opinion," or "economic decline," or "political power," enter into general propositions of far lesser range or dependability than any in even the least developed natural science. Such historical generalizations turn out, for the most part, to be tautologous, or vague or inaccurate: "All power tends to corrupt"; "Every revolution is followed by a reaction"; "Industrialization radically alters artistic taste" will yield, taken with some specified initial conditions, e.g. "Cromwell had absolute power" or "a revolution broke out in Russia in 1917," scarcely any reliable concrete deductions. What is here conspicuously lacking is an interconnected tissue of generalizations which an electronic brain could mechanically apply to a situation mechanically specifiable as relevant. What actually occurs in historical thinking is much more like the operation of common sense, where we weave together various logically independent concepts and general propositions, and bring them to bear on a given situation as best we can. The capacity to do this successfully—the ability to "weave together," "bring to bear" various concepts—is an intuitive (and empirical) knack—often called judgment—which electronic brains cannot be given by their manufacturers.

L. At this point we may be told that the mysterious capacity of weighing or assessing a concrete situation, the arts of diagnosis, of prognosis—the so-called faculty of judgment—is not unique to history and the other humane studies, or to thinking and decision-making in ordinary life; for in the natural sciences too, the capacity for perceiving the relevance of one, rather than another, theory or concept to the solution of a given problem, and the "bringing to bear" upon a given body of data of notions sometimes derived from very remote fields, is nothing if not the peculiar skill of a gifted individual, sometimes amounting to the insight of genius, which techniques or machines cannot in principle be made to replace. This is true, yet there exists one striking difference between the canons of explanation and logical justification used by the sciences and the humanities, that will serve to emphasize the chasm between them. In a developed work of natural science—say, a textbook of physics or biology (I do not refer to speculative or impressionistic discourses which are to be found in scientific treatises)—the links between the propositions are, or should be, logically obvious: the propositions follow from each other; that is to say, the conclusions are seen logically to follow from premises either with demonstrative certainty, or else with varying degrees of probability which, in the sciences which use statistical methods, should be capable of being estimated with a fair degree of precision. Even if such symbols of inference as "because," or "therefore," or "hence" were omitted, a piece of reasoning in mathematics or physics or any other developed natural science (if it were clearly set out) would exhibit its inner logical structure by the sheer meaning and order of its component propositions. As for the propositions that are stated without argument, these are, or should be, such that, if challenged, their truth or probability could be demonstrated by recognized logical steps from truths established experimentally and accepted by virtually all the relevant specialists. This is very far from being the case in even the best, most convincing, most rigorously argued works of history. No student of history can, I think, fail to note the abundance, in works of history, of such phrases as "small wonder if," "it was therefore hardly surprising when," "the inevitable consequences swiftly followed," "events took their inevitable course," "from this it was but a short step to," and most often of all, the scarcely noticeable, indispensable and deeply treacherous "thus," "thereupon" and the like. If these bridges from one set of facts or statements to another were suddenly withdrawn from our textbooks, it is, I think, not too much to say that the transition from one set of statements to the other would become a great deal less smooth: the bald juxtaposition of events or facts would at times be seen to carry no great logical force in itself, and the best constructed cases of some of our best historians (and lawyers) would begin—to minds conditioned by the criteria of natural science—to seem less irresistible.

I do not mean to imply that the humanities, and particularly history, take in their readers by a species of confidence trick—by simulating the outer shell, the logical structure, of scientific method without its substance; only that the force of such convenient, and perhaps indispensable, links as "because" and "therefore," is different in the two spheres; each performing their own legitimate—and parallel—functions, and leading to difficulties only if they are (mistakenly) regarded as performing logically identical tasks in both spheres. This point will, I hope, become clearer still if it is developed.

M. Let us assume that an historian who is attempting to discover and explain the course of a large historical phenomenon, such as a war or a revolution, is pressed to state those laws and general propositions which alone (at least in theory) could justify his constant use of such logical links as "hence," "therefore," or expressions like "the unavoidable result was," "from this there was no turning back" and the rest of his stock in trade, what could his answer be? He might hesitantly trot out some general maxims about the influence of environment or a particular state of affairs—a bad harvest, or an inflationary spiral, or a wound to national pride—as it affects men in general or a specific group of human beings in particular; or he might speak about the influence of the interests of this or that class or nation, or the effect of religious convictions or social habits or political traditions. But if he is then pressed about the evidence for these generalizations; and upon marshaling what he can, is then told that no self-respecting science would tolerate so vague, unsifted and above all exiguous a body of factual evidence, nor such impressionistic methods of rveying it or deriving conclusions from it in disregard of the elementary rules of inductive and deductive reasoning, he would not (if he were honest or wise) insist on claiming the authority of a fully-fledged natural science for his activity. At this point someone might quite correctly point out to him that not all social sciences are in so deplorable a condition; that, for example, there exist disciplines—economics is perhaps the best known—where something resembling scientific procedure does appear to take place. In economics concepts can, we are assured, be defined with a fair measure of precision: there is distinct awareness of the differences between definitions, hypotheses and inductive generalizations; or between the empirical evidence and the conclusions drawn from it; or between the model and the reality to which it is applied; or between the fruit of observation and that of extrapolation, and so forth. This is then held up as a model to the unfortunate historian, wandering helplessly in his dark and pathless wood. Yet if he tries to follow the advice of the friends of enlightenment —sociologists, social psychologists, doctrinaire Marxists, positivists, theorists of history, and the like—his progress is soon arrested. Attempts to provide history with laws have taken two main directions: all-embracing schemata, and division into specialized disciplines. The first has given us the systems of historiosophers, culminating in the vast edifices of Hegel, Spengler, Toynbee and the like, which are found to be too general and vague to be informative on anything in particular, and at times neither accurate nor plausible in matters of detail when their evidence is tested by exact scholars in the relevant fields. The second path leads to monographs about selected aspects of human activity— for example, the history of technology, or of the evolution of a given science or art or social activity, which do indeed satisfy some of the criteria of natural scientists, but only at the expense of leaving out the greater part of what is known of the life of the human beings whose histories are in this way recorded.

Any attempt to "integrate" these isolated strands, treated by the special disciplines, into something approaching a "total" description of human experience—of what, in Aristotle's words, "Alcibiades did and suffered"—comes up against an insurmountable obstacle: that the facts to be fitted into the scientific grid and subsumed under inductive laws (even if public criteria for selecting what is important, relevant, etc. from what is trivial, peripheral, etc., can be found and employed) are too many, too minute, too fleeting, too blurred at the edges. They crisscross and penetrate each other at many levels simultaneously, and the attempt to prise them apart, as it were, and pin them down, and classify them, and fit them into their specific compartments, turns out to be impracticable. Wherever efforts to pursue this policy have been pressed with real vehemence—by those who were obsessed with the dominant role of some one factor, as Buckle was by that of climate, or Taine by his trinity of the *milieu,* the moment and the race, or Marxists by that of the class struggle—they lead to obvious distortions, and the results, even when they contain illuminating ideas and *aperçus,* are liable to be rejected as being over-schematized, that is, as being too unlike human life as we know it.

The fact that this is so, seems to me of cardinal importance and to carry a crucial implication. For one of the central differences between such genuine attempts to apply scientific method to human affairs as are embodied in, say, economics or social psychology or sociology, and the analogous attempt to apply it in history proper, is this: that scientific procedure is directed in the first place to the construction of an ideal model, with which the portion of the real world to be analyzed must, as it were, be matched, so that it can be described and analyzed in the terms of its deviation from the model. But to construct a useful model will only be feasible when it is possible to abstract a sufficient number of sufficiently stable similarities from the things, facts, events, of which the real world—the flow of experience—is composed. Only where such recurrences in the real world are frequent enough, and similar enough to be classifiable as so many deviations from the selfsame model, will the idealized model that is compounded of them —the electron, the gene, the economic man—do its job of making it possible for us to extrapolate from the known to the unknown. It follows from this that the greater the number of similarities[3] we are able to collect (and the more dissimilarities we are able to ignore) that is to say, the more successfully we abstract, the simpler our model will be, the narrower will be the range of characteristics to which it will apply, and the more precisely it will apply to it; and, conversely, the greater the variety of objects to which we want our model to apply, the less we shall be able to exclude, and, consequently, the more complex the model will become and the less precisely it will fit the rich diversity of objects which it is meant to summarize, and consequently the less of a model, of a master key, it will necessarily be. A theory festooned with *ad hoc* hypotheses to account for each specific deviation from the norm will, like Ptolemy's epicycles, soon cease to be useful. Exclusion—neglect of what is beyond the defined frontiers—is entailed in model-building as such. Hence it begins to look as if, given the world as it is,[4] the applicability of a theory or a model tends to vary directly as the number of cases, and inversely with the number of characteristics, which it covers. Consequently one may, at times, be compelled to choose between the rival rewards of increased extension or intension—between the number of entities to which a theory applies, and the richness of the content of the entities. The most rigorous and universal of all models is that of mathematics, because it operates at the level of the highest possible abstraction from

---

[3] Or at best significant similarities, that is, those in which we are interested.

[4] It might have been different; if it possessed fewer characteristics and these coexisted or recurred with much greater uniformity and regularity, the facts of history could be reduced to a natural science or sciences. Human experience would then be unimaginably different.

natural characteristics. Physics, similarly, ignores deliberately all but the very narrow group of characteristics which natural objects possess in common, and its power and scope (and its great triumphs) are directly attributable to its rejection of all but certain selected ubiquitous and recurrent similarities. As we go down the scale, sciences become richer in content and correspondingly less rigorous, less susceptible to quantitative techniques. Economics is a science precisely to the degree to which it can successfully eliminate from consideration those aspects of human activity which are not concerned with production, consumption, distribution, etc. The attempt to eliminate from the consideration of economists psychological factors, such as, for instance, the springs or the varieties of human actions, or the purposes or the states of mind connected with them; or to exclude moral considerations such as, for example, the respective values of motives and consequences, or of individual and group satisfaction—such procedure is wholly justified so long as its sole aim is to render economics as much of a science as possible: that is to say, an instrument capable of analysis and prediction. If anyone then complains that economics, so conceived, leaves out too much, or fails to solve some of the most fundamental problems of individual and social welfare—among them questions which had originally stimulated this science into existence—one is entitled to reply that the omitted sides of life can be accommodated, and moral, psychological, political, metaphysical questions can perhaps be answered, but only at the price of departing from the rigor and the symmetry—and predictive power—of the models with which economic science operates; that versatility, richness of content, capacity to deal with many categories of problems, adaptability to the complexities of widely varying situations—all this may be purchasable only at the expense of logical simplicity, coherence, economy, width of scope and, above all, capacity to move from the known to the unknown. These latter characteristics, with which Newtonian physics had, understandably enough, hypnotized the entire intellectual world, can only be obtained by drawing precise frontiers for a given activity and ruthlessly casting out (so far as possible) whatever has not been provided for in this specification. It is for this reason that even in the case of the more descriptive and time-bound disciplines, the more general and rigorous the concepts involved and the more "technical" the approach, the better able they are to use methods similar to those of the natural sciences; the more elastic its concepts and the richer their content, the remoter from a natural science such a discipline will be.

If this is true, then Comte was not altogether mistaken: mathematics, physics, biology, psychology, sociology, are indeed rungs in a descending order of comprehensiveness and precision, and in an ascending order of concreteness and detail. General history—the richest of all human studies—shows this very plainly. If I am purely an economic historian, I can probably establish certain generalizations about the behavior of some commodity—say wool—in some portion of the Middle Ages, for which enough documentary evidence exists to enable me to establish correlations between the production, sale, distribution of wool, etc., and certain related social and economic facts and events. But I am able to do this only by refusing to attend to questions about other aspects of the wool producers or wool merchants—I do not attempt to establish measurable correlations of the sources and movements of the bales of wool with the religious, or moral, or aesthetic attitudes of wool growers or wool users, or their political ideals, or their conduct as husbands or citizens or churchmen. For this reason, I find it useful to employ technical terms (always symptomatic of the fact that a model is at work) in an artificially delimited field—namely that of economic history. The same considerations apply, for example, to the history of technology, or of mathematics, or of clothing, and the like. I construct the model by abstracting; by noting only what, say, industrial techniques, or mathematical methods, or methods of composing music, have in common, and constructing my model solely out of these common characteristics, however much of general interest I may be leaving out. The more I wish to put in, the more overweighted and, in due course, cluttered up and shapeless, my model is bound to become, until it is scarcely a model at all, for it no longer covers a sufficient number of actual and possible cases in a sufficient variety of places and times. Its utility will steadily diminish.

N. The proposition that sciences deal with the type, not the individual, was accepted and indeed insisted upon by those philosophical historians, particularly in France, who desired to assimilate their activities to those of scientists. When Renan, or Taine, or Monod preached the necessity of scientific history, they did not merely mean that historians should seek to be precise, or exercise rigor in observation or reasoning, or apply the findings of the natural sciences to the explanation of human action or experience wherever possible, or that they should grind no axe but that of objective truth, and state it without qualification whatever the moral or social or political consequences. They claimed much more. Taine, in his *Histoire: son Présent et son Avenir,* states this point of view clearly, when he declares that historians work with samples:

What was there in France in the eighteenth century? Twenty

million men . . . twenty million threads the crisscrossing of which makes a web. This immense web, with innumerable knots, cannot be grasped clearly in its entirety by anyone's memory or imagination. All we have is mere fragments . . . the historian's task is to restore them—he reconstructs the wisps of the threads that he can see so as to connect them with the myriad threads that have vanished. Fortunately in the past, as now, society included groups, each group consisting of men who were like one another—born in the same condition, molded by the same education, moved by the same interests, with the same needs, same tastes, same *moeurs,* same culture, same basis to their lives. In seeing one, you have seen all. In every science we study each class of facts by means of chosen samples. . . . Let us enter into the private life of a man (typical of his time after we have studied him minutely) . . . We shall understand the force and direction of the current that carries forward the whole of his society. The monograph is the historian's best tool: he plunges it into the past like a lancet and draws it out charged with complete and authentic specimens. One understands a period after twenty or thirty such soundings: only they must be carried out and interpreted rightly.

This is a characteristic of the high tide of positivist optimism in which truth is mixed with error. No doubt it is true that our only key to understanding a culture or an age is by the detailed study of the lives of representative individuals or families or groups. We cannot examine all the acts and thoughts of all (or even a large number) of the human beings alive during the age in question (or any other age): we generalize from samples. We integrate the results of such generalizations into what Taine calls the total "web." In "reconstructing" the "vanished threads," we make use of chemistry, astronomy, geology, paleontology, epigraphy, every scientific method known to us. But the objective of all this is to understand the relation of parts to wholes, not, as Taine believed, of instance to general law. In a natural science—zoology and economics alike—our aim is to construct a model ("the mammal," "the monopolistic firm") which we can apply, with which we can reach out into the unknown past or future with a fair degree of confidence in the result; for the central criterion of whether or not a study is a true science, is its capacity to infer the unknown from the known. The process that Taine describes is not this at all; it is reconstruction in terms of a pattern, an interrelated social whole, obtained from "entering into" individual human lives, provided that they turn out to be "typical"—that is, significant or characteristic beyond themselves. The sense of what is characteristic and representative, of what is a true sample suitable for being generalized, and, above all, of how the generalizations fit in with each other—that is the exercise of judgment, a qualitative, quasi-intuitive form of thinking dependent on wide experience, memory, imagination, on the sense of "reality," of what goes with what, which may need control by, but is not at all identical with, the capacity for logical reasoning and the construction of laws and scientific models—the capacity for perceiving the relations of particular case to law, instance to general rule, theorems to axioms, not of parts to wholes or fragments to completed patterns. I do not mean that these are incompatible "faculties" capable of functioning in isolation from each other—only that the gifts are dissimilar, and determine different approaches to the world, and that Buckle and Comte and Taine and Marx and their modern disciples, when they bandy the word "scientific," do not perceive this, and lead men astray.

O. Let me put this in yet another way. Every student of historiography knows that many of the major achievements of modern historians come from their practice of certain rules, which the more reflective among them sometimes express in advice to practitioners of this craft. Historical students are told not to pay too much attention to personal factors or heroic and unusual figures in human history. They are told to attend to the lives of ordinary men, or to economic considerations or social factors or irrational impulses or traditional and unconscious springs of action; not to forget such impersonal, inconspicuous, dull, slowly or imperceptibly altering factors of change, as erosion of the soil, or systems of irrigation and drainage, which may be more influential than spectacular victories, or catastrophic events, or acts of genius; they are told not to allow themselves to be carried away by the desire to be entertaining or paradoxical, or over-rationalistic, or to point a moral or demonstrate a theory; and much else of this kind. What justifies such maxims? They do not follow from the rules of the deductive or inductive disciplines; they are not even rules of specialized techniques (like, say, the *a fortiori* principle in rhetoric, or that of *difficilior lectio* in textual criticism). What logical or technical rules can be laid down for determining precisely what, in a given situation, is due to rational or purposive, and what to "senseless" or irrational factors, how much to personal action, how much to impersonal forces? If anyone supposes that such rules can be drawn up, let him attempt to do so. It seems plain that the maxims are nothing but distillations of generalized sagacity—of practical judgement founded on observation, intelligence, imagination, on empirical insight, knowledge of what can and what cannot be, something that resembles a skill or gift more than factual knowledge[5] but is not iden-

---

[5] See pp. 96-97 and pp. 105-106 below.

tical with either; guides of the highest value to action (in this case, to mental labor) which scientific techniques can aid, sharpen, criticize, correct, but never replace.

P. This is but another way of saying that the business of a science is to concentrate on similarities, not differences, to be general, to omit everything that is not relevant to answering the severely delimited questions that it permits itself to ask. But those historians who are concerned with a field wider than the specialized activities of men, are interested precisely in that which differentiates one thing, person, situation, age, pattern of experience, individual or collective, from another; when they attempt to account for and explain, say, the French Revolution, the last thing that they seek to do is to concentrate only on those characteristics which the French Revolution has in common with other revolutions, to abstract only common recurrent characteristics, to formulate a law on the basis of them, or at any rate an hypothesis, from which something about the pattern of all revolutions as such (or, more modestly, all European revolutions) and therefore of this revolution in particular, could in principle be reliably inferred. This, if it were feasible, would be the task of sociology, which would then stand to history as a "pure" science to its application. The validity of the claim of sociology to be a natural science is another story, and not directly related to history, whose tasks are different. The purpose of historians, as has often been repeated, is to paint a portrait of a situation or a process, which, like all portraits, seeks to capture the unique pattern and peculiar characteristics of its particular subject; not to be an X-ray which eliminates all but what a great many subjects have in common. This has often been said, but its bearing on the possibility of transforming history into a natural science has not always been clearly perceived.

Q. One way of appreciating this contrast is by contrasting two uses of the word "because." Max Weber, whose discussion of this problem is extraordinarily illuminating, asked himself, under what conditions I accept an explanation of a given individual action or attitude as adequate, and are these conditions the same as those that are required in the natural sciences?—that is to say, he tried to analyze what is meant by rational explanation in these two contrasted fields. If I understand him correctly, he argues somewhat as follows: Supposing that a doctor informs me that his patient recovered from pneumonia because he was injected with penicillin, what rational grounds have I for accepting this "because"? My belief is rational only if I have rational grounds for believing the general proposition "penicillin is effective against pneumonia," a causal proposition established by experiment and observation, which there is no reason to accept unless, in fact, it has been arrived at by valid methods of scientific inference. No amount of general reflection would justify my accepting this general proposition (or its application in a given case) unless I know that it has been or could be experimentally verified. The "because" in this case is a symbol indicating a claim that a *de facto* correlation between penicillin and pneumonia has, in fact, been established. I may find this surprising or I may not; this does not affect its reality: scientific investigation—inductive or hypothetical-deductive—establishes its truth as a fact; and that is the end of the matter. If, on the other hand, I am told, in the course of an historical narrative (or in a work of fiction, or ordinary life) that X resented the behavior of Y, because X was weak and Y was arrogant and strong; or that X forgave the insult he had received from Y, because he was too fond of Y to feel aggrieved; and if, having accepted these "because" statements as adequate explanations of the behavior of X and Y, I am then challenged to produce the general law which I am leaning on, consciously or not, to "cover" these cases, what would it be reasonable for me to reply? I may well produce something like "the weak often resent the arrogant and strong," or "human beings forgive insults from those they love." But supposing I am then asked what concrete evidence I have for the truth of these general propositions, what scientific experiments I or anyone else have performed to establish these generalizations, how many observed and tested cases they rest on—I may well be at a loss to answer. Even if I am able to cite examples from my own or others' experience of the attitude of the weak to the strong, or of the behavior of persons capable of love and friendship, I may be scornfully told by a psychologist—or any other devotee of strict scientific method—that the number of instances I have produced is ludicrously insufficient to be adequate evidence for a generalization of such scope; that no respectable science would accept these few instances which, moreover, have not been observed under scientific conditions, as a basis for serious claims to formulate laws; that such procedures are impressionistic, vague, pre-scientific, unworthy to be reckoned as ground for a scientific hypothesis. And I may further be told that what cannot enter a natural science cannot be called fully rational but only an approximation to it (an "explanation sketch"). Implicit in this approach is Descartes' criterion, the setting up of the methods of mathematics (or physics) as the standard for all rational thought. Nevertheless, the explanation that I have given in terms of the normal attitude of the weak to the strong, or of friends to one another, would, of course, be accepted by most rational beings (writers and readers of history among them) as an adequate explanation of the behavior of a given individual in the relevant situation. This kind of explanation may not be admissible in a treatise on natural science, but in dealing with others, of describing their actions, we accept it as being both normal and reasonable; neither as inescapably shallow, or unexamined, or doubtful, nor as necessarily needing support from the laboratory. We may, of course, in any given case, be mistaken—mistaken about particular facts to be accounted for, the attitude of the relevant individuals to one another, or in taking for granted the generalizations implicit in our judgment; these may well be in need of correction from a science such as psychology or sociology. But because we may be in error in a given instance, it does not in the least follow that this type of explanation is always systematically at fault, and should or could be replaced by something more searching, more inductive, more like the type of evidence that is alone admitted in, say, biology. If we probe further and ask why it is that such explanations—such uses of "because"—are accepted in history, and what is meant by saying that it is rational to accept them, the answer must surely be that what in ordinary life we call adequate explanation often rests not on a specific piece of scientific reasoning, but on our experience in general, on our understanding of the habits of thought and action that govern human attitudes and behavior, on what is called knowledge of life, sense of reality. If someone tells us, "X forgave Y because he loved him," or "X killed Y because he hated him," we accept these propositions easily, because they fit in with our general experience, because we claim to know what men are like, not, as a rule, by careful observation of them as psychological specimens (as Taine recommends), or as members of some strange tribe whose behavior is obscure to us and can only be inferred from observation, but because we claim to know what—in essentials—a human being is, in particular a human being who belongs to a civilization not too unlike our own, and consequently one who thinks, wills, feels, acts in a manner which (rightly or wrongly) we assume to be intelligible to us because it sufficiently resembles our own or those of other human beings whose lives are intertwined with our own. This sort of "because" is the "because" neither of induction nor of deduction, but the "because" of understanding—*Verstehen*—of recognition of a given piece of behavior as being part and parcel of a pattern of activity which we can follow, which we can remember or imagine, and which we describe in terms of the general laws which cannot all, or even for the most part, be rendered explicit (still less organized into a system), but without which the texture of human life—all that we call social or personal reality—is not conceivable. We may make mistakes; or we may be shallow, unobservant, naïve, unimaginative, not allow enough for unconscious motives, or unintended consequences, or the play of chance or some other factor; we may project the present into the past or assume uncritically that the basic categories and concepts of our civilization apply to remote or dissimilar cultures, which they do not fit. But although any one explanation or use of "because" and "therefore" may be rejected or shaken for any of these or a hundred other reasons, all such explanations cannot be rejected *in toto* in favor of inductive procedures derived from the natural sciences, because that would cut the ground from beneath our feet: the context in which we think, act, expect to be understood or responded to, would be destroyed. When I understand a sentence which someone utters, I know what he means not in virtue of inductively reached knowledge that the statistical probability that the noises he emits are, in fact, connected and expressive in the way that I take them to be—knowledge based on comparison of the sounds he utters with a great many other sounds that a great many other beings have uttered in corresponding situations in the past. Nor, if I were called upon to justify my assertion that I understand what he is saying, could I, as a rule, produce an impressive piece of inductive reasoning in its favor, although no doubt, if pressed, I could conduct an experiment which would do at any rate something to support my belief. Nevertheless, my belief is much stronger than any process of reasoning that I may have performed with a view to bolstering it up would, in a natural science, be held to justify. Yet we do not for this reason regard such claims to understanding as being irrational or arbitrary. When I say that I realize that X forgave Y because he loved him or was too good-natured to bear a grudge, what I am ultimately appealing to is my own (or my society's) experience and imagination, my (or my associates') knowledge of what such relationships can be. This knowledge, whether it is my own, or taken by me on trust—accepted uncritically—may often be inadequate, and I may commit blunders, but if all such knowledge were rejected unless it could pass scientific tests, I could not think or act at all.

R. The world of natural science is the world of the external observer noting as carefully and dispassionately as possible the compresence or succession (or lack of it), or degrees of correlation of empirical characteristics. In formulating a scientific hypothesis, I must, at least in theory, start from the initial assumption that, for all I know, anything might occur next door to, or before or after, or simultaneously with, anything else; nature is full of surprises; I must take as little as possible for granted; it is the business of a natural science to establish general laws recording what most often or invariably does occur. But in human affairs, in the interplay of men with one another, of their feelings, thoughts, actions, ideas about the world or each other or themselves, it would be absurd (and if pushed to extremes, impossible) to start in this manner. I do not start from an ignorance which leaves all doors—or as many of them as possible—open, for here I am not primarily an external observer, but myself an actor; I understand other human beings, and what it is to have motives, feelings, or to follow rules, because I am human myself, and because to be active, that is, to want, intend, make plans, speculate, react to others self-consciously, be aware of my situation *vis-à-vis* other conscious beings (as well as nature,) is *eo ipso* to be engaged in a constant fitting of fragments of reality into the single all-embracing pattern that I assume to hold for others besides myself, and which I call reality. When, in fact, I am successful in this—when the fragments seem to me to fit—we call this an explanation; when in fact they do fit, I am called rational; if they fit badly, if my sense of harmony is a delusion, I am called irrational, fanciful, distraught, silly; if they do not fit at all, I am called mad.

S. So much for differences in method. Besides this there is also a profound difference of aim between scientific and historical studies. What they seek for is not the same. Let me illustrate this with a simple example. Supposing that we look at an average, unsophisticated European or American school text of modern European history, that offers a sample of the kind of elementary historical writing upon which most of us have been brought up. Let us consider the kind of account that one finds in routine works of this type, of, say, the causes of the French Revolution. It is not unusual to be told that among its causes were—to give the headings —(i) the oppression of French peasants by the aristocracy, the Church, the King, etc.; (ii) the disordered state of French finances; (iii) the weak character of Louis XVI; (iv) the subversive influence of the writings of Voltaire, the Encyclopedists, Rousseau, and so on; (v) the frustrated ambitions of the French *bourgeoisie,* barred from their proper share of political power; and so forth. One may reasonably protest against the crudity and naïveté of such treatments of history: Tolstoy has provided some very savage and entertaining parodies of it and its practitioners. But if one's main anxiety is to convert history into a science, one's indignation should take a different and much more specific form. One should declare that what is here manifested is a grotesque confusion of categories, an outrage to scientific method. For the anlysis of the condition of the peasants belongs to the science of economics, or perhaps of social history; that of French fiscal policy to the science of public finance, which is not primarily an historical study, but one founded on timeless principles; the weakness of the King's character is a matter for individual psychology (or biography); the influence of Voltaire and Rousseau belongs to the history of ideas; the pressure of the middle classes is a sociological topic, and so forth. Each of these disciplines must surely possess its own methods, canons, concepts, categories, logical structure. To heap them into one, and reel off a list of causes, as if they all belonged to the same level and type, is intellectually scandalous: the rope composed of these wholly heterogeneous strands must at once be unwound, each of the strands must then be treated separately in its proper logical box. Such should be the reaction of someone who takes seriously the proposition that history is, or at any rate should be, a natural science or a compound of such sciences. Yet the truth about history—perhaps the most important truth of all—is that history *is* precisely this amalgam, a rich brew composed of apparently disparate ingredients, that we do in fact think of these different causes as factors in a single unitary sequence—the history of the French nation during a particular segment of time—and that whatever merit there may be in detaching this or that element of a single process for analysis in a specialized laboratory, yet to treat them as if they were genuinely separate, insulated streams which do not compose a single river, is a far wilder departure from what we think history to be, than the indiscriminate compounding of them into one string of causes, as is done in the simple-minded schoolbooks. "History is what historians do," and what historians aim at is to answer those who wish to be told what important changes occurred in French public life between 1789 and 1794, and why they took place. We wish, ideally at least, to be presented, if not with a total experience—which is a logical as well as a practical impossibility—at least with something full enough and concrete enough to meet our conception of public life (itself an abstraction, but not a deductive schema, not an artificially constructed model) seen from as many points of view and at as many levels as possible, including as many components, factors, aspects, as the widest and deepest knowledge, the greatest analytic power, insight, imagination, can present. If we are told that this cannot be achieved by a natural science—that is, by the application of models to reality, because models can only function if their subject matter is "thin" and consists of deliberately isolated strands of experience, and not "thick" in the texture constituted by the interwoven strands—then history is not in this sense a science; a narrowly scientific cast of mind is seldom found together with historical curiosity or historical talent. We can make use of scientific techniques to establish dates, order events in time and space, exclude untenable hypotheses and suggest new explanatory factors, but the function of all these techniques, indispensable as they are today, can be no more than ancillary, for they are determined by their specific models, and are consequently "thin," whereas history is necessarily "thick": that is its essence, its purpose and its reason for existence.

T. History, and other accounts of human life, are at times spoken of as being akin to art; and what is usually meant is that writing about human life depends to a large extent on skill in describing, on style, lucidity, choice of examples, distribution of emphasis, vividness of characterization, and the like. But there is a profounder sense in which the historian's activity is an artistic one. Historical explanation is to a large degree arrangement of the discovered facts in patterns which satisfy us because they accord with life as we know it and can imagine it. That is the difference that divides human studies—*Geisteswissenschaften*—from those of nature. When these patterns employ concepts or categories that are ephemeral, or confined to trivial or unfamiliar aspects of human experience, we speak of such explanations as shallow, or inadequate, or eccentric, and find them unsatisfactory on those grounds. When these concepts are of wide implication, permanent, familiar, common to many men and many civilizations, we experience a sense of reality and dependability that derives from this very fact, and regard the explanation as well-founded, serious, satisfactory. On some occasions, seldom enough, the explanation not only involves, but reveals, basic categories of universal import, which, once they are forced upon consciousness, we recognize as underlying all our experience; yet so closely interwoven are they with all that we are and feel, and therefore so totally taken for granted, that to touch them at all is to communicate a shock to the entire system; the shock is one of recognition and one that may upset us, as is liable to happen when something deep-set and fundamental that has lain unquestioned and in darkness, is suddenly illuminated or prised out of its frame for closer inspection. When this occurs we call such explanations profound, fundamental, revolutionary, and those who proffer them—Vico, Marx, Freud—men of depth or insight or genius.

U. This kind of historical explanation is akin to moral and esthetic analysis, because it presupposes understanding of human beings not merely as bodies in space, obeying causal laws, but as active beings, willing, creating, pursuing ends, shaping their own and others' lives, reflecting, imagining, in constant interaction with other human beings, engaged in all the forms of experience that we understand only by being ourselves involved in them, and not as external observers. This is what is called the inside view: it is explanation whose primary function is not to predict or extrapolate, but fit the loose and fleeting objects of sense, imagination, intellect, into the central succession of patterns that we call normal, and which is the ultimate criterion of reality as against illusion, incoherence, fiction. History is merely the projection into the past of this activity of selection and adjustment, the search for coherence and unity, together with the attempt to refine it with all the self-consciousness of which we are capable, by bringing to its aid everything that we conceive to be useful—all the sciences, all the knowledge and skills that we have acquired, from whatever quarter. This, indeed, is why we speak of the importance of allowing for imponderables in forming historical judgment, or of the quasi-mysterious faculty of judgment that is not obviously useful in chemistry or algebra; of the importance of common sense, or knowledge of life, or width of experience, or breadth of sympathy or imagination, or natural wisdom, or "depth" of insight, none of which have central importance for physicists or geologists. Capacity for understanding peoples' characters, knowledge of ways in which they are likely to react to one another, ability to "enter into" their motives, their principles, the "inward" movement of their spirit (and this applies no less to the behavior of masses or to the growth of cultures)—these are the gifts that are indispensable to historians, but not, or not to such a degree, to natural scientists. The historian's primary need is the knowledge that is like knowledge of someone's character or face, not like knowledge of facts. Without knowledge of facts, an historical construction may be no more than a coherent fiction, a work of the romantic imagination; it goes without saying that if it is to be true, it must be tethered to reality by verification of the facts, as in any natural science. Nevertheless, even though in this ultimate sense what is meant by real and true is identical in science, in history and in ordinary life, yet the differences remain at least as great as the similarities.

V. This notion of what historians are doing when they explain may cast light also upon something that was mentioned earlier; namely, the idea of the inexorable succession of the stages of development, which made it not merely erroneous but absurd to suppose that *Hamlet* could have been written at the court of Genghis Khan, or that Richelieu could have pursued the policies realized by Bismarck. For this is not something that we derive from a careful inductive investigation of conditions in Outer Mongolia, as opposed to those of Elizabethan England, or the political relations between the great powers in the nineteenth century as opposed to those in the seventeenth, but from a more fundamental sense of what goes with what. We conceive of historical succession as being akin to that of the growth of the individual mind; to suggest that a child thinks or wills or acts like an old man, or *vice versa,* is something that we reject on the basis of our own direct experience (I mean not introspection, but knowledge of life—something that springs from interaction with others and with the surrounding environment and constitutes the sense of reality). Our conception of a civilization is analogous to this. We do not feel it necessary to enumerate all the specific ways in which a wild nomad differs from a European of the Renaissance, or ask ourselves why it is—what inductive evidence we have for the contingent proposition that—the culture of the Renaissance is not merely unlike, but represents a more mature phase of human growth than, that of Outer Mongolia during the times of Genghis Khan. The proposition that the culture of the Renaissance not merely did not precede, but cannot have preceded, the nomadic stage in the continuous development that we call a single culture, is something so intrinsic to our conception of how men live, of what societies are, of how they develop, that it is a presupposition of our investigations and not their goal or product, and is therefore logically not in need of justification by their methods or results. For this reason one might hesitate to call such knowledge empirical, for it is not confirmable or corrigible by the normal empirical methods, to which it functions as base—as a frame of reference; but neither, of course, is it *a priori* (as Vico and Hegel, who showed original insight into this matter, sometimes imply) if by that is meant that it is obtainable in some special, non-naturalistic way. Recognition of the fundamental categories of human experience differs from both empirical information, and deductive reasoning: they underlie both, and are the least changeable elements in our knowledge. Yet they can alter: and above all, we can ask ourselves to what degree this or that conceivable change in them would affect our experience. Moreover it is possible, although *ex hypothesi* not easy, to conceive of beings whose fundamental categories of thought or perception radically differ from ours; the greater such differences, the harder it will be for us to communicate with them, or, if the process goes farther, to regard them as being human; or, if the process goes too far, to conceive of them at all.

W. It is a corollary of this that one of the difficulties that beset historians, and do not beset natural scientists, is that of reconstructing what occurred in the past, not merely in terms of our own concepts and categories, but also of how such events must have looked to those who participated or were affected by them—psychological facts that in their turn themselves influenced events. It is difficult enough to develop an adequate consciousness of what we are and what we are at, and how we have arrived where we have done, without also being called upon to make clear to ourselves what such consciousness and self-conciousness must have been like for persons in situations different from our own; yet no less is expected of the true historian. Chemists and physicists are not obliged to investigate the states of mind of Lavoisier or Boyle; still less of the unenlightened mass of men. Mathematicians need not worry themselves with the general outlook of Euclid or Newton. Economists need not know the inner vision of Adam Smith or Keynes or their less gifted contemporaries. But it is the inescapable business of the historian to ask himself not merely what occurred (in the sense of publicly observable events), but also how the situation looked to various representative Greeks or Romans, or to Alexander or Julius Caesar, and above all to Thucydides, Tacitus or anonymous medieval chroniclers, or to Englishmen or Germans in the sixteenth century, or Frenchmen in 1789 or Russians in 1917, or to Luther, or Cromwell, or Robespierre or Lenin. This kind of imaginative projection of ourselves into the past, the attempt to capture concepts and categories not altogether like ours by means of concepts and categories that cannot but be our own, is a task that we can never be sure that we are even beginning to achieve, yet are not permitted to abjure. We seek to apply scientific tests to our conclusions, but this will take us but a little way. For it is a commonplace by now that the frontiers between fact and interpretation are blurred and shifting, and what is fact from one perspective, is interpretation from another. Even if chemical and paleographic and archeological methods yield some hard pebbles of indubitable fact, the task of interpretation cannot be evaded; and nothing counts as an historical interpretation unless it attempts to answer the question of how the world must have looked to individuals or societies if their acts and words are to be taken as the acts and words of human beings neither wholly like ourselves nor so different as not to fit into our common past. Without a capacity for sympathy and imagination beyond any required by a physicist, there is no vision of either past or present, neither of others nor of ourselves; but without this, normal—as well as historical—thinking cannot function at all.

X. The contrast which I am trying to draw is not the difference between the two permanently opposed but complementary human demands: one for unity and homogeneity, the other for diversity and heterogeneity, which Kant has made so clear.[6] The contrast I mean is one between different types of knowledge. When the Jews are enjoined in the Bible to protect strangers, "For ye know the soul of a stranger, seeing ye were strangers in the land of Egypt" (Ex. 23:9), this knowledge is neither deductive, nor inductive, nor founded on direct inspection, but akin to the "I know" of "I know what it is to be hungry and poor," or "I know how political bodies function," or "I know what it is to be a Brahmin." This is neither (to use Professor Gilbert Ryle's useful classification) "knowing that" which the sciences provide, nor the "knowing how" which is the possession of a disposition or skill, nor the knowledge of direct perception, acquaintance, memory, but the knowledge that an administrator or politician must possess of the men with whom he deals. If the historian is endowed with this too poorly, if he can fall back only on inductive techniques, then, however accurate his discoveries of fact, they remain those of an antiquarian, a chronicler, at best an archeologist, but not those of an historian. Perhaps some light may be cast on this by comparing historical method with that of linguistic or literary scholarship. No scholar could emend a text without a capacity (for which no technique exists) for "entering into the mind of" another society and age. Electronic brains cannot perform this: they can offer alternative combinations of letters but not choose between them successfully. How do gifted scholars in fact arrive at their emendations? They do all that the most exacting natural science would demand: they steep themselves in the material of their authors; they compare, contrast, manipulate combinations like the most accomplished cypher breakers; they may find it useful to apply

---

[6] *Critique of Pure Reason*, ed. Cassirer, III, 455.

statistical and quantitative methods; they formulate hypotheses and test them; all this may be indispensable but it is not enough. In the end what guides them is a sense of what a given author could, and what he could not, have said; of what fits and what does not fit, into the general pattern of his thought. This, let me say again, is not the way in which we demonstrate that penicillin cures pneumonia.

Y. The deepest chasm which divides historical from scientific studies is between the outlook of the external observer and that of the actor. It is this that was brought out by the contrast between "inner" and "outer" (which Vico initiated, and after him, the Germans), between the questions "How?" or "What?" or "When?" on one side, and the questions "Why?," "Following what rule?," "Towards what goal?," "Springing from what motive?" on the other. It lies in the difference between the category of mere togetherness or succession (the correlations to which all sciences can in the end be reduced), and that of coherence and interpretation; between factual knowledge and understanding. The latter alone makes intelligible that celebrated identity in difference (which many of the Idealist philosophers exaggerated and abused) in virtue of which we conceive of one and the same outlook as being expressed in very diverse manifestations, perceive affinities (that are often difficult and at times impossible to formulate) between the dress of a society and its morals, its systems of justice and the character of its poetry, its architecture and its domestic habits, its sciences and its religious symbols. This is Montesquieu's "spirit" of the laws (or institutions) that belong to a society. Indeed, this alone gives its sense to the very notion of belonging;[7] without it we should not know what is meant when we speak of something as belong-

---

[7] Cf. p. 70 above.

ing to, or being characteristic or typical of an age or a style or an outlook, or conversely of some interpretation as involving an anachronism—an incompatibility between a given phenomenon and its alleged context in time; immediate awareness of this type is different in kind from awareness of a formal contradiction between theories or propositions. Historical sense—a concentrated interest in particular events or persons or situations as such [8] is a prerequisite of that historical sense which, like sense of occasion in agents intent on achieving some specific purpose, is sharpened by love or hate or danger; it is this that guides us in understanding, discovering and explaining. When historians assert particular propositions like "Lenin played a crucial role in making the Russian Revolution," or "Without Churchill England would have been defeated in 1940," the rational grounds for such assertions, whatever their plausibility, are not identical with generalizations of the type "Such men, in such conditions, usually affect events in this fashion" for which the evidence may be exceedingly feeble; for we do not test them solely—or indeed generally —by their logical links with such general propositions, but rather in terms of their coherence with our picture of a specific situation; to analyze this type of knowledge into a finite collection of general and specific, categorical and

---

[8] "There are really only two ways of acquiring knowledge of human affairs," said Ranke, "through the preception of the particular or through abstraction.... The former is the method of history. There is no other way.... Two qualities, I think, are required for the making of the true historian: first he must feel a participation and pleasure in the particular for itself.... Just as one takes delight in flowers without thinking to what genus of Linnaeus ... they belong, without thinking how the whole manifests itself in the particular.

"Still this does not suffice; ... while [the historian] reflects on the particular, the development of the world in general will become apparent to him." Quoted in *The Varieties of History,* ed. Fritz Stern (New York, 1956), 58–59.

hypothetical propositions is certainly not practicable. Every judgment that we formulate, whether in historical thought or ordinary life, involves general ideas and propositions without which there can be no thought or language. At times some among these generalizations can be clearly formulated, and combined into models; where this occurs, natural sciences arise. But the descriptive and explanatory language of historians, because they seek to deal with the specific or even unique phenomena in concrete detail,[9] cannot be successfully reduced to such general formulae, still less to models and their applications. Any attempt to do so will be halted by the discovery that the subject matter involves a thick texture of crisscrossing, constantly changing and melting conscious and unconscious beliefs and assumptions some of which it is difficult or impossible to formulate, on which our rational views and rational acts are founded, or which they exhibit or express. This is the "web" of which Taine speaks, and it is possible to go only some way (it is impossible to say in advance how far) towards isolating and describing its ingredients if our rationality is challenged. And even if we succeed in making explicit all (which is absurd) or many of our general propositions or beliefs, this achievement will not take us much nearer the scientific ideal: for between a collection of generalizations—or unanalyzed knots of them—and the construction of a model there still lies difficult or impassable country: the generalizations must exhibit an exceptional degree of constancy and logical connection, if this passage is to be accomplished.

What are we to call the faculty which an artist displays

---

[9] All facts are, of course, unique, those dealt with by natural scientists no less than any others; but it is not their uniqueness that interests scientists. I owe this point to Professor H. L. A. Hart.

in choosing his material and knowing how to realize his purpose by means of it, which a politician needs when he makes a decision whose success may depend on the degree of his sensitiveness to the circumstances, the human characters, the interplay between them, with which, and upon which, he is working? The *Wirkungszusammenhang,* the sense of the general structure of experience—that is the pattern, understanding of which may indeed be useful to scientists but which is absolutely indispensable to historians. Without it, they remain chroniclers or technical specialists. They may achieve accuracy, objectivity, lucidity, literary quality, breadth of knowledge, but unless they convey a vision of life, and exhibit a semi-intuitive sense of what fits with what, of a *Gestalt* not, as a rule, capable of being formalized in terms say, of a field theory, the result is not recognized by us as an account of reality—that is, of what human beings, as we understand the term, could have felt or thought or done.

It was, I think, Professor Namier who once remarked about historical sense that there was no *a priori* shortcut to knowledge of the past; what actually happened can only be established by scrupulous empirical investigation, by research in its normal sense. What is meant by historical sense is the knowledge not of what happened, but of what did not happen. When an historian in attempting to decide what occurred and why, rejects all the infinity of logically open possibilities, the vast majority of which are obviously absurd, and, like a detective, investigates only those possibilities which have at least some initial plausibility, it is this sense of what is plausible—what men, being men, could have done or been—that constitutes the sense of coherence with the patterns of life that I have tried to indicate. Such words as plausibility, likelihood, sense of reality, historical sense, are typical qualitative categories which distinguish historical studies as opposed to the natural sciences that seek to operate on a quantitative basis. This distinction, which originated in Vico and Herder and was developed by Dilthey and Weber, is of fundamental importance.

Z. The gifts that historians need are different from those of the natural scientists. The latter must abstract, generalize, idealize, quantify, dissociate normally associated ideas (for nature is full of strange surprises, and as little as possible must be taken for granted), deduce, establish with certainty, reduce everything to the maximum degree of regularity, uniformity, and, so far as possible, to timeless repetitive patterns. Historians cannot ply their trade without a considerable capacity for thinking in general terms; but they need, in addition, peculiar attributes of their own: a capacity for integration, for perceiving qualitative similarities and differences, a sense of the unique fashion in which various factors combine in the particular concrete situation, which must at once be neither so unlike any other situation as to constitute a total break with the continuous flow of human experience, not yet so stylized and uniform as to be the obvious creature of theory and not of flesh and blood. The gifts needed are those of association, not dissociation, of perceiving the relation of parts to wholes, of particular sounds or colors to the many possible tunes or pictures into which they might enter, of the links that connect individuals viewed and savored as individuals and not as instances of types or laws. These gifts relate more directly to practice than to theory. A man who lacks common intelligence can be a physicist of genius, but not even a mediocre historian. The characteristics indispensable to historians are more akin to those needed in active human intercourse, than in the study or the laboratory or the cloister. The capacity for associating the fruits of experience in a manner that enables its possessors to distinguish, without the benefit of rules, what is central, permanent or universal from what is local, or peripheral or transient—that is what gives concreteness and plausibility, the breath of life, to historical accounts. Skill in verifying facts by means of observation or memory or inductive procedures, while indispensable to the discovery of all truth about the world, is not the rarest quality required by historians, nor is the desire to find recurrences and laws a mark of historical talent.

If we ask ourselves what historians have commanded the most lasting admiration, we shall, I think, find that they are neither the most ingenious, nor the most precise, nor even the discoverers of new facts or causal connections, but those who (like imaginative writers) present men or societies or situations in many dimensions, at many intersecting levels simultaneously, writers in whose accounts human lives, and their relations both to each other and to the external world, are what (at our most lucid and imaginative) we know that they can be. The gifts that scientists most need are not these: they must be ready to call everything into question, to construct bold hypotheses unrelated to empirical procedures, and drive their logical implications as far as they will go, free from control by common sense or too great a fear of departing from what is normal or possible in the world. Only in this way will new truths and relations between them be found—truths which, as in physics or mathematics, do not depend upon the peculiarities of human nature and its activity. In this sense, to say of history that it should approximate to the condition of a science is to ask it to contradict its essence.

It would be generally agreed that the reverse of a grasp

of reality is the tendency to fantasy or utopia. But perhaps there exist more ways than one to defy reality. May it not be that to be unscientific is to defy, for no good logical or empirical reason, established hypotheses and laws; while to be unhistorical is the opposite—to ignore or twist one's view of particular events, persons, predicaments, in the name of laws, theories, principles derived from other fields, logical, ethical, metaphysical, scientific, which the nature of the medium renders inapplicable? For what else is it that is done by those theorists who are called fanatical because their faith in a given pattern is not overcome by their sense of reality? For this reason the attempt to construct a discipline which would stand to concrete history as pure to applied, is not a vain hope for something beyond human powers, but a chimera, born of a profound incapacity to grasp the nature of natural science, or of history, or of both.

The Historian's Use of Nationalism and *Vice Versa*

DAVID M. POTTER

David M. Potter was born in Augusta, Georgia in 1910, and took his undergraduate degree at Emory University (1932) and his doctorate at Yale (1940). He began his career as a teacher of American history in 1936 at the University of Mississippi, moving to the Rice Institute (now Rice University) in 1938. In 1942 he became a member of the history department at Yale, where he was advanced to a professorship in 1949 and where he remained until 1961. Since then he has been William R. Coe, Professor of American History at Stanford University. In 1947–1948 he was Harmsworth Professor of American History at Oxford. He held the Walgreen lectureship at Chicago in 1950 and is scheduled to hold the Commonwealth lectureship at University College, London in 1963.

Although Professor Potter has done intensive work on the antecedents of the Civil War (Lincoln and His Party in the Secession Crisis, *and in other writings) and on the study of national character as applied to the American people* (People of Plenty, *among other writings), he has sought to be a generalist more than a specialist. Since 1957, he has been a member of the Committee on Historical Analysis of the Social Science Research Council, whose aim is a more systematic approach to the problem of the nature of historical generalizations.*

It is one of the basic characteristics of history that the

historian is concerned with human beings but that he does not deal with them primarily as individuals, as does the psychologist or the biographer or the novelist. Instead he deals with them in groups—in religious groups, as when he is concerned with the wars of the sixteenth century; in cultural groups, as when he is treating the broad history of civilizations; in ideological groups, as in the conflict between pragmatists and idealists; in interest groups, such as the landed interest or the monied interest; in occupational groups, such as the farmers and the ranchers; or in social groups, such as the gentry and the yeomanry. But most often the historian deals with people in national groups. These national groups usually coincide with a political state; but it would be too restrictive to say that the national group is simply a political group, for very often the historian is not concerned with the political aspects of the history of the group. As a social historian, for instance, he may be interested in the social development of the American people or the English people, and may be quite indifferent to the history of the United States or of Britain as a political entity. Similarly, if he is an intellectual historian, his field of inquiry may be the history of American thought or of British thought—again without any concern for governmental aspects.

Just as the rise of nationalism has been the major political development of modern times, so attention to the national group, rather than to these other groupings, has correspondingly become perhaps the major focus of modern historians. Accordingly, the identity of people in terms of their nationality has grown to transcend all other identities, so that we speak and think constantly in terms of the American people, the Japanese people, the Russian people, and so on. Our attribution of distinctive traits and attitudes, reactions and values, to these groups shows that we do not conceive of them merely in political terms as bodies who happen to be subject to a common political jurisdiction, but rather as aggregations whose common nationality imparts or reflects an integral identity. The idea that the people of the world fall naturally into a series of national groups is one of the dominating presuppositions of our time. For the historian it takes the form of a basic, almost an indispensable generalization, so that even historians who recognize that exaggerated nationalism is one of the greatest evils of the modern world, still are very prone to conceive of the structure of the world in national terms.

Because of the constant, pervasive use of this criterion of nationality as the basis for classifying the two and a half billion members of the world's population, the concept of nationality has become a crucial one in modern historical thought, with many far-reaching implications. It is the purpose of this essay, therefore, to explore some of the implications which reside in the historian's concept of nationalism, some of the unrecognized side effects which the concept, with its attendant ideas, has had, and something of the way in which it has affected the treatment of history.

Perhaps the most crucial fact in shaping the historian's use of the idea of nationalism is that he employs it in two quite distinct ways for two different purposes. On the one hand, he uses it in answering a question as to the degree of cohesiveness or group unity which has developed in a given aggregate of people. Here the question is primarily descriptive or observational, and it can be answered in qualified or relative terms, or in terms of degree, with fine distinctions and gradations. Such a question may concern the psychological attitudes of the group, and in fact the prevailing theory of nationalism today emphasizes its psychological character. Thus, for example, Hans Kohn affirms that "nationalism is first and foremost a state of mind, an act of consciousness," and, though he points out that one must also explain the surrounding conditions which produce the state of mind, he accepts as valid, though limited, the statement that a nation is "a group of individuals that feels itself one [and] is ready within limits to sacrifice the individual for the group advantage."[1] Proponents of this psychological view recognize, of course, that a subjective group-feeling is a phenomenon not likely to develop unless there are objective conditions which give rise to it. Conceivably in theory, a group of people might form a nation simply by believing passionately enough that they shared qualities in common, even if this belief were an illusion. But this is only in theory, and in fact nearly all authorities on nationalism have given a great deal of emphasis to the objective or substantive conditions from which the sense of common identity is derived. Such conditions include the sharing of a common language, the occupation of a territorial area which constitutes a natural unit (an island, a river valley, or mountain-girt basin), the adherence to a common religion, and a heritage of common mores and traditions. But these factors in themselves are not regarded as components of nationality. They are rather prerequisites or raw materials, conducive to the development of the psychological manifestation.

The psychological character of this approach to nationalism deserves emphasis because it carries with it certain important corollaries. It would follow, to begin with, that since nationalism is a form of group loyalty, it is not generically different from other forms of group loyalty.

---

[1] Hans Kohn, *The Idea of Nationalism: A Study in its Origins and Background* (New York, 1944), 10–20, esp. 10, 12.

From this it would follow further that nationality is not an absolute condition, but a relative one, for loyalty evolves gradually by imperceptible degrees, both in the individual and in the group; it ebbs and flows; and it is modified by contingencies. If nationalism is a relative manifestation, this fact would also imply that various national groups must vary in the degree of completeness or intensity of their nationality, and further that various elements of the population within the nationality group must vary in the extent to which they share the sense of group identity and the commitment to the group purpose. This, in turn, would mean that loyalty to the nation must exist in the individual not as a unique or exclusive allegiance, but as an attachment concurrent with other forms of group loyalty—to family, to church, to school and to the individual's native region. Since it exists concurrently, it must also, as has been suggested, partake of the nature of these other forms of loyalty.

All of these corollaries are accepted, explicitly or implicitly, by most writers on nationalism. They are consonant with the theory which writers have found most tenable, and when historians are directly engaged in the specific study of the growth of nationalism, their analysis usually gives due weight to the variable, impalpable, evolutionary and sometimes partially developed nature of the manifestations of nationalism. In such a context, the historian seldom loses sight of the fact that nationalism is a tendency, an impulse, an attitude of mind, rather than an objective, determinate thing.

If the historian had only to deal with the question of the extent to which a group has become national, he would probably never treat it in other terms than these, which are so consistent with his theory and with his general disposition to take a functional rather than a formalistic view of historical phenomena.

But in another—a second—aspect, the historian uses the concept of nationalism in answering a second question which frequently arises in history, as to the validity of a given group's exercising autonomous powers. In human affairs, society has long since agreed to the proposition that when a multiplicity of individuals stand in a certain relation to one another—or to put it more concretely, when they form a community—they incur certain obligations toward one another which they would not have if they were not a community, and that the community has a "right," or enjoys a sanction, to enforce these obligations and to defend itself as a community, if necessary by the use of coercion and violence—which would otherwise be taboo. But the sanction to exercise these powers and the determination of whom they can rightfully be exercised upon— individuals or minority groups—depends entirely upon whether the body seeking to exercise them and the individuals upon whom they are to be exercised form a true community. Thus, the nature of the relation between the individuals involved, rather than the ethical character of the acts performed, actually becomes the standard for judging the rightfulness of the acts. Here the nation occupies a particularly crucial role, for of all human communities it is the one to which this power of regulation, control, coercion, punitive action and so on, is especially assigned. Therefore in any given case where a body of people contests the exercise of authority by another body over it (and history is full of such cases), the crucial question is fundamentally whether the two are parts of a single community, or, more specifically, a single nation, in which case the exercise is valid; or whether they belong to separate communities, or nations, in which case it is not valid. In such a case, the determination of nationalism ceases to be a merely descriptive matter; it becomes an evaluative matter, for the attribution of nationality sanctions the acts of the group claiming autonomous powers. Further, this determination cannot be made by psychological analysis, which offers only relativistic, qualified, balanced terms, and does not yield yes-or-no, all-or-nothing answers. Such analysis can tell what measure of nationality a group has attained, for that is a question of degree; but it cannot determine whether the group has attained the measure of nationality appropriate to the exercise of national powers, for that is a categorical or classificatory question. The categorical nature of the problem he is dealing with, therefore, tends to draw the historian unconsciously away from his theory. Where his theory tells him that nationalism is a relative thing, existing in partial form, his practice may impel him to treat it as an absolute thing, existing in full or not at all. (For instance, national loyalty may vary enormously, or in subtle degrees, but national citizenship does not vary at all—a man is a citizen or he is an alien.) Where his theory emphasizes the view that national loyalty is a form of group loyalty, and generically similar to other forms of group loyalty, his practice impels him to treat it as a unique form of devotion, potentially antithetical to other forms of loyalty such as regional loyalty. (He even uses a different word for this loyalty—the word "allegiance"). Where his theory recognizes that nationalism is a form of emotion, and that, like other forms of emotion, it will attain varying degrees of intensity in varying segments of the population, his practice is to treat it as a matter of standard, fixed specifications (the citizen is either "loyal" or is "disloyal").

Thus, the shift from a descriptive to a classificatory approach is also a shift from a psychological (or functional) approach to an institutional (or formalistic) approach. It is a deceptively easy and, at times, almost imperceptible shift to make, because the nation is, of course, in an extremely real and important sense, an institutional thing. The impulse of nationalism fulfills itself in the formation of the national institutions, and while a nation is truly a body of people who feel themselves to be one, it is also, quite as truly, the organized body of people who share this feeling, together with the organization which the feeling prompts them to set up.

But though these two concepts flow rather naturally into one another, they are in many ways inconsistent with and even antithetical to one another. One treats the nation as an abstraction having no physical reality (only on a political map, which is itself an abstraction, is it possible to see where one nation ends and another begins). But institutionally, the nation assumes all the concreteness which a census of population, an inventory of resources, an army and navy, and all the apparatus of public authority can give to it. In psychological terms, a nation exists only subjectively, as a focus of men's loyalties; without these loyalties there would be no nation. But once the nation has been institutionalized, men tend to regard the institution itself as transcendent—a thing to which the loyalties of men ought to be given simply because it does exist. Again, in theory, the nation survives as a unit because people continue to feel a psychological unity. But in operative terms, its survival may depend upon the power of the state to override divisive impulses and to control an aggregation of people as if they were one, even despite a significant degree of reluctance on the part of some of those who are being thus united.

In short, the institutional view does violence to the historian's theory, for it pulls him in the direction of treating nationality as objective rather than subjective, absolute rather than relative, and total rather than partial. It also impels him to isolate it from and place it in antithesis to other forms of group loyalty, instead of keeping in view the fact that the psychological ingredients of nationalism are the same as for other forms of human identification with large groups. Finally, and most important, it leads him to give a valuative, rather than a purely descriptive property to his attribution of nationality.

The political state as we know it today possesses tremendously powerful devices for making the institutional aspects of nationality seem more real than the psychological aspects. With the paraphernalia of symbols (the flag, the crown, the national anthem, the constitution) it evokes the emotional responses of patriotism. By such means as citizenship, territorial boundaries and sovereignty *vis-à-vis* other political states, it sets up demarcations which separate and even differentiate humans beings on one side of an imaginary geographical line from human beings on the other side of this line. Even though it should be situated upon a terrain which lacks any natural geographical unity, it can employ the concept of a "common territory" so persuasively as to create the illusion of commonality for geographically diverse areas, whereas, in the absence of common political jurisdiction, real features of geographical unity will not be recognized as the basis for a commonality. As Karl Deutsch has suggested, there is no reasoning more circular than the argument that Detroit and San Francisco, for instance, are "united" by lying within a "common territory," while Detroit and Toronto are "separated" by not lying in a common territory.[2]

In the same way, although a state may have a population which is varied and lacking in homogeneity, it can bring the concept of a "common citizenship" to bear. By this concept it can create the illusion of an affinity between individuals whose interest may be in conflict, whose cultures may be diverse, and whose values may be antagonistic, while it inhibits the full recognition of features of commonality between individuals who do not share the same citizenship.

To say this is, of course, not to deny that most political states are based upon very real factors of nationality which make for their separateness and identity. The congruence of the nation and the political state is, indeed, very complete in many cases, for political nationality tends to follow cultural boundaries when it is forming and to reinforce the cultural separateness of a national population after it has formed. But the operative importance of formalistic features such as citizenship, jurisdiction, territoriality and so on, tends to convey an image of nationality which is far more institutional than psychological. And this concept is, of course, far more categorical, more absolute, more unitary in its implications: the individual either is or is not a citizen; the public authority either does or does not have jurisdiction; the disputed area lies either inside or outside of the national boundary. None of these matters are partial, any more than sovereignty itself is partial—and sovereignty, it used to be said, is like virginity in that it cannot be surrendered in part.

---

[2] Karl W. Deutsch, *Nationalism and Social Communication: An Inquiry into the Foundations of Nationality* (New York and London, 1953), 4.

The sheer weight and momentum of modern institutional nationalism makes it difficult for the historian to resist the institutional concept, especially when this concept is, in certain respects, entirely valid and realistic. He is himself, after all, not only an historian but also a "national" of one or another nation; he is the creature of an age which tends to reify the nation, the inhabitant of a globe which is commonly believed to be composed of one hundred and three "nations" more or less—each with one vote in the U.N., and therefore each, as a nation, interchangeable with each other nation. In theory, he knows that there is a great difference between the nation and the political state, but in a world where all the states claim to be nations and all the nations try to be states, it is difficult for him to remember that they are two things. When he is offered a complete set of "nations" neat in order, precise in outline, manageable in number and all alphabetically arranged in the *World Almanac,* it requires a real effort of imagination and even of will on his part to think of the world as composed of inchoate, amorphous congeries of human beings, confused in their groupings and indeterminate in their alignments, and overwhelming in their number.

Nevertheless, historians are now to some extent on guard against mistaking the nation as a people for the nation as a state. Certainly most treatises on nationalism warn them against confusing nationality itself with the forms which the nationalistic impulse has projected.[3] But they are often not on guard against the subtle shift from describing the nationalistic impulse as a socio-psychological phenomenon to using the attribution of nationalism as a valuative device. For it is a paradox not generally recognized that

---

[3] Kohn, *op. cit.,* 18–20; Carlton J. Hayes, *Essays on Nationalism* (New York, 1928), 4–5.

the historian cannot make a simple descriptive observation about the degree of group cohesion among an aggregate of people without inadvertently registering a valuative judgment as to the validity of the powers which this aggregation may assert for itself. If he were applying a standard of ethics, it would be recognized at once as a valuative standard, but since he seemingly applies only a measure of relationships, it is easy to overlook the valuative implications. Yet the concept of the nature of the group may be more crucial than the concept of right and wrong in determining the validity of acts committed in the name of nationality. For even the Declaration of Independence did not proclaim the right of everyone to resist tyranny, but rather the right of "one people to dissolve the political bonds which have connected them with another." The separability of "one people" and "another" was a necessary prerequisite to the dissolution of the bonds. Conversely, a belief that bonds ought to be dissolved would make it necessary to believe also that the Americans were "one people" and the British "another."

Indeed modern democratic thought, by adopting the view that the ultimate authority lies in the people, has brought us to the point where the nature of the association which constitutes a people takes on almost as mystical a quality as once pertained to the nature of the anointment which a crowned king received from God. For the major premise of democracy, that the majority shall rule, is predicated upon the assumption that some larger whole, recognizable both by those persons who are imposing their will on the one hand, and by those who are submitting to the imposition on the other, really does exist. Unless the minority really is identified with and part of such a whole, the decisions of the majority lack any democratic sanction.

For instance, if the Magyars under Louis Kossuth were a "people," they were morally justified in their "revolution" against the old Austro-Hungarian Empire; they were "patriots"; and their uprising was a "war of independence." But if not, they were morally censurable for "rebelling", they were "traitors"; and their uprising was an "insurrection." If the Croats who, in turn, fought against Kossuth's authority were a "people," then Kossuth was a "tyrant," and his measures against them were "acts of oppression"; but if not, he was merely a resolute leader defending his "nation" against "disruptive elements" that sought to "subvert" it. There is hardly any historical situation for which semantics are more crucial: Indeed, where the concept of nationality is involved, the virtue or the evil of a man's act may not be determined by the character of the act itself, nor even by the motives for which it is executed, but entirely by the status of the group in whose behalf it is undertaken.

In sum, when the historian attributes nationality to any group, he establishes a presumption in favor of any acts involving an exercise of autonomy which the group may commit; when he denies nationality, he establishes a presumption against any exercise of autonomy. The attribution of nationality therefore involves a sanction—a sanction for the exercise of autonomy or self-determination.[4]

Of all the consequences of the shift toward an institutional concept, this insertion of the valuative or sanctioning implication has had, perhaps, the most sweeping consequences. Indeed, the element of sanction is almost the essence of this concept. It carries with it some far-reaching implications, and these implications have had such perva-

---

[4] Rupert Emerson, in *From Empire to Nation: The Rise to Self-Assertion of Asian and African Peoples* (Cambridge, Mass., 1960), 134, speaks of the nation as "the community which legitimizes the state."

sive effects upon the interpretation of history that it becomes important to examine and recognize them.

To begin with, it is fundamental that once nationality is conceived to imply rights or powers for the national group, and not merely to describe the degree of cohesiveness within that group, the historian will begin to be influenced in his reasoning not only by his observations about the degree of cohesion, but also by his beliefs about the justice or the merits of the group's claim to autonomy. Instead of arguing forward, therefore, from the observation that the evidence indicates a high degree of psychological coherence (nationality), and that consequently the group was justified in acting as a nation, he may be tempted to argue backward, from the conviction that since the group was, in his opinion, justified in exercising national powers, it must have had, psychologically, a high degree of cohesiveness. What appears on its face to be a mere observational or descriptive statement about psychological attitudes may be in fact an indirect form of argumentation about the validity of a set of political claims.

In other words, the writer who is trying to rationalize a position need no longer do so with legal or ethical arguments, which are the normal medium of rationalization. Instead, he is likely to rationalize it in terms of cultural and psychological analysis, applying a criterion of relationship rather than a criterion of ethics.

On the surface, it often appears today that the nineteenth-century writer on nations who used to argue freely in abstract and formalistic terms—about "compact," "sovereignty" and the like—has been replaced in the twentieth century by a writer who takes a functional approach, tracing the gradual cultural development by which a "people" become self-consciously united, and measuring the extent of governmental power in terms of the degree of social need. But to an astonishing degree, the old formalism and the new functionalism come to the same thing. In the past, the ultimate sanction for a government was the possession of sovereignty; today its ultimate sanction is that it acts for a population which constitute a "people" in the special sense which entitles them to self-determination. But the effect, in either case, is to ascribe indirectly a right to the exercise of autonomy.

A second implication of the valuative aspect of nationalism is that it inhibits the historian's recognition of the generic similarity between national loyalty and other forms of group loyalty. It does this because national loyalty, in its valuative sense must be singular, if not indeed unique. This inhibition cuts off a number of useful insights. It prevents the historian from seeing that in situations where nationalism and sectionalism are both at work, they are not necessarily polar or antithetical forces, even though circumstances may cause them to work in opposition to one another. Nationalism, in fact, may be the terminal result of a full development of strong sectional forces, while sectionalism may be an emergent nationalism which has not yet matured.

At a deeper level, this inhibition may blind the historian to the fact that national loyalty, far from being opposed to other loyalties, is in fact strengthened by incorporating them. Harold Guetzkow, in discussing the creation of international loyalties, makes this point clearly: "The behaviorist leads us to believe that strong family, local and national loyalties are helpful in building international loyalties. The analyst assures us that loyalty is attachable to various objects—an international object as well as a national object. If loyalty is a generalized way of responding, the stronger the loyalty pattern in a given individual—no matter what its object—the easier it will be to build loyalties." Guetzkow also quotes the blunter statement of A. M. Rose that "people can have loyalty to two [or more] groups or two sets of values, even when these groups or values are in conflict." [5]

Going a step beyond Guetzkow, Morton Grodzins argues in *The Loyal and the Disloyal,* that other loyalties not only are conducive to strong national loyalty, but are even indispensable to it. "Other loyalties," he says "are . . . the most important foundation of democratic national loyalty. . . . The welter of non-national loyalties makes a direct national loyalty a misnomer. It does not exist. Loyalties are to specific groups, specific goals, specific programs of action. Populations are loyal to the nation as a by-product of satisfactions achieved within non-national groups, because the nation is believed to symbolize and sustain these groups. From this point of view, one is loyal not to nation but to family, business, religion, friends. One fights for the joys of his pinochle club when he is said to fight for his country." [6]

Historians frequently write about national loyalty as if it were exclusive, and inconsistent with other loyalties, which are described as "competing" or "divided," and which are viewed as detracting from the primary loyalty to the nation. Yet it is self-evident that national loyalty flourishes not by

---

[5] Harold Guetzkow, *Multiple Loyalties* (Princeton, 1955), 37, 39. Also, Merle Curti in *The Roots of American Loyalty* (New York, 1948), 47, says, "Local and regional loyalties did not necessarily conflict with loyalty to the nation."

[6] Morton Grodzins, *The Loyal and the Disloyal: Social Boundaries of Patriotism and Treason* (Chicago, 1956), 29. See also *id.,* "The Basis of National Loyalty," *Bulletin of the Atomic Scientists,* VII (Dec. 1951), 356–62.

challenging and overpowering all other loyalties, but by subsuming them all in a mutually supportive relation to one another. The strength of the whole is not enhanced by destroying the parts, but is made up of the sum of the parts. The only citizens who are capable of strong national loyalty are those who are capable of strong group loyalty, and such persons are likely to express this capacity in their devotion to their religion, their community and their families, as well as in their love of country. The nationalism which will utilize this capacity most effectively, therefore, is not the one which overrides and destroys all other objects of loyalty, but the one which draws them all into one transcendent focus. A well-known phrase runs, "for God, for Country, and for Yale"—not "for God, or Country, or for Yale."

A third implication of the evaluative aspect of nationalism is that it sometimes impels the historian to deny nationality to groups of whom he morally disapproves, even though the group may in every sense fulfill his theoretical criteria of nationality. For instance, if a fascist group should claim a separate nationality, the historian, in theory, need only ask whether the members of the group do in fact feel themselves to be one and whether the regime which they are setting up is established "with the consent of the governed." But in fact he can scarcely accord nationality to a group without also seeming to accord some degree of sanction to the cause for which the group stands—namely the cause of fascism. Since he is reluctant to do this, he tends, as a lawyer would say, to "distinguish" the case and to rationalize a basis for denying the nationalism of the group in question. Most historians, if confronted with the abstract proposition that people who practice wrong cannot be united by deep cultural commonalities, would dismiss it as absurd. Yet the functional implications of the concept of nationalism are such that historians in fact are frequently unwilling to recognize cultural commonalities of this kind in the case of groups whose values they reject.

A fourth warping result of the same evaluative tendency is the belief that nationality must be based upon peculiarly deep-seated cultural affinities among a people, since only such fundamental ties would justify the kind of power and unique autonomy which is ascribed to the national group. No trivial or unworthy grounds for association could justify a group in claiming the kind of immunity from external control, and power to abuse internal minorities, which are accorded to a nation. Therefore, when the historian is faced with manifestations of nationalism, he will, almost by reflex, begin his analysis of these manifestations by searching for profound common elements in the culture of the group involved. Indeed, there is a standard formula, accepted by all the authorities on the subject, which enjoins him to give his attention to "certain objective bonds [which] delimit a social group, [such as] common descent, language, territory, political entity, customs and tradition, and religion." [7] Accordingly, students of nationalism have emphasized the growth of the vernacular languages in Western Europe; they have ransacked folklore and the popular culture for any features which illustrate a common tradition among the people. Also they have often treated the territorial area which finally eventuated, no matter how fortuitously, from any nationalist movement, as the logical fulfillment of a

---

[7] Kohn, *The Idea of Nationalism*, 13–14, 6–10. These criteria, so clearly stated by Kohn, are not distinctly his, but are standard criteria among students of nationalism. For a critique of the "illusions concerning the basis of nations and nationalism," however, see Boyd C. Shafer, *Nationalism: Myth and Reality* (New York, 1955), 13–56.

mystic impulse among the folk to unite a "common territory." The true believer who found it an evidence of divine providence that all our seaports have harbors evinced no greater faith than the historian who defines all the land within a given national jurisdiction as a "common territory" and then uses the assumption that it is a common territory to prove the validity of the national jurisdiction.

This does not mean, of course, that the common cultural factors are not real or, in many cases, of immense importance. Indeed, some of the oldest and most famous nations —England, Japan and France, among others—lend support to the contention that a population isolated by physical or linguistic or other barriers may develop an extremely clear-cut cultural identity, which may prove by far the most enduring and most cohesive basis of nationality.

But the very preoccupation of historians with classic examples such as these has perhaps led them to overemphasize the cultural component of nationality,[8] and to assume too simple an equation between nationality and culture. There is, of course, no doubt that commonalities in culture have a primary role in generating the spirit of nationalism, but secondarily there is also the reverse effect that movements for political statehood, which are commonly regarded as nationalist movements, tend to claim commonalities of culture as a sanction for their objectives; and if these cultural elements do not exist in reality, the nationalist movement may fabricate them. It is notorious, for instance, that Gaelic was culturally a dying speech in Ireland, and Welsh a dying speech in Wales, and that both have received

---

[8] Emerson (*From Empire to Nation*, 103) comments that "theoretical approaches to the concepts of nation and nationalism have been dominated by the European experience, even though this European-derived framework fitted the facts in much of the rest of the world in only indifferent fashion at the best."

a somewhat artificial rejuvenation because of the zeal of Irish and Welsh nationalists.[9]

In this instance, we are confronted by common cultural factors that are attentuated, yet still very real. But it has seemed increasingly evident in the last quarter of a century that many "nationalist" movements have a minimum of common cultural content and that the impulse which moves them is primarily a negative political reaction against an existing regime (especially a colonial regime). For instance, some of the new nations of Africa appear to consist of territories which, instead of coinciding with any unified culture areas of their own, correspond to the administrative divisions laid down for purposes of bureaucratic convenience by their former colonial masters. It is perhaps the final irony of European colonialism that it is likely to fix the patterns and alignment of the nationalism which replaces it and utterly repudiates it.[10] When a new "nation" is being

---

[9] Shafer (*Nationalism*, 189) remarks that "within groups not yet nations, linguistic studies were the first signs of a rising national consciousness. They were also consciously made to stimulate it." On the Welsh language, artificially sustained, see Sir Reginald Coupland, *Welsh and Scottish Nationalism: A Study* (London, 1954), 357–66.

[10] Emerson (*op. cit.*, 60) observes: "Indeed, the creation of nations themselves is in some instances, as in the Philippines and Ghana, to be attributed primarily to the bringing together of diverse stocks under a single imperial roof. . . . Uncertain as the precise meaning of the term 'national character' may be, it is beyond doubt that the character of the nations now coming into the world has been greatly influenced by the type of colonial regime to which they have been subjected." The heavily negative character of nationalism in modern Africa is suggested by Thomas Hodgkin, *Nationalism in Colonial Africa* (New York, 1956), 21–23, when he asks, "At what stage is it reasonable to describe a movement of colonial protest or opposition to European authority as 'nationalist' in respect of its aims and character?" and answers, "My own inclination is to use the term nationalist in a broad sense to describe any organization or group that explicitly asserts the rights, claims, and aspirations of a given African society (from the level of the language group to that of Pan-Africa) in opposition to European authority, whatever its institutional form and objectives."

formed in such circumstances, it will behoove the leaders to claim for their country all the attributes which have been regarded as giving a sanction to the older and more organic nations. If the highest of all sanctions—a national culture—is lacking, the spokesmen of the "nationalism" in question will be impelled to fabricate or simulate the cultural factors which are needed as proofs of the validity of their nation. Such simulation will, indeed, not be anything new, for the spokesmen of nationalism have always exaggerated the degree of separateness and coherence of the national group, even in the oldest and most fully defined nations, and these nations have always relied upon a certain amount of carefully cultivated mythology to reinforce the unity of their people. Their success in fostering a belief in a common identity has often been an essential part of the process of forging the identity itself; the belief has operated as a kind of self-fulfilling prophecy. If the members of a population are sufficiently persuaded that they have cause to be a unified group, the conviction itself may unify them, and thus may produce the nationalism which it appears to reflect.

But while it is to be expected that nationalist leaders will if necessary contrive a synthetic culture for a particular state, it is all the more vital that the historian should be forever alert to distinguish between a genuine culture generating a genuine nationalism, and a trumped-up nationalism generating the pretense or illusion of a culture. Yet there are certain prevailing traits among historians which limit their capacity to maintain this distinction. For one thing, the historian's conviction that he has a professional duty to ransack all the sources for every scrap of evidence means that he will usually find some data, no matter how tenuous, which can be construed to "prove" the existence of the pretended culture. Further, the historian is not only an historian; he is also a man and a citizen, and his national loyalties as a citizen may sometimes neutralize his impartiality as an historian; it is well known that history has often been a handmaiden of patriotism. Finally, the examples of nationalism which have dominated the historical imagination are deeply-rooted, clearly-defined, long-sustained nations, and this very preoccupation prompts the historian to think of nationalism as the outgrowth of a cultural group identity of unique depth and pervasiveness—in short, to regard nationalism simply as an aspect of culture. This impulse accords well with his deep-seated moral feeling that no entity ought to enjoy the sanctions which pertain to nationality, unless it is based upon a deeply rooted culture.

To repeat, then, the historian has an extremely strong predisposition to equate nationality and culture. This predisposition is so strong that if other important sources of nationalism should exist, recognition of them would be inhibited under our present rationale of nationalism. A question arises, therefore, whether other important sources of nationalism do exist, and if so, what their nature may be.

There is certainly at least one other important factor beside common culture which may bind an aggregate of individuals together, and this is community of interest, not in the narrow sense of economic advantage only, but in the broad sense of welfare and security through membership in society. It is axiomatic that people tend to give their loyalty to institutions which "protect" them—that is, safeguard their interests—and political allegiance throughout history has been regarded as something given reciprocally in return for protection. Historians have clearly recognized this relationship, and one may add that historians of nationalism have often called attention to it. Thus, when modern nationalism was in its infancy, Voltaire defined the word *patrie* in terms of community of interest. Among modern historians, Hans Kohn affirms that a nationality derives part of its strength from being regarded as "a source of economic well being"; Karl Deutsch states that when he and his collaborators were "studying cases of successful amalgamation" of diverse groups into a single nation, "they found that it was apparently important for each of the participating territories or populations to gain some valued services or opportunities"; Boyd Shafer is particularly explicit in pointing out that for many nationalists "devotion to the national welfare . . . after all was but devotion to their own welfare," that monarch and middle classes at the inception of modern nationalism "found mutual benefit in the joint extension of their mutual interests, which they also could conceive of as *the* national interests," and that these parties were like "stockholders with voting rights in the common enterprise, the nation." One of the clearest affirmations of this idea was made by Harry M. Schulman in a statement to Louis L. Snyder, quoted in Snyder's *The Meaning of Nationalism.* Nationalism, said Schulman, is not a *we*-sentiment, but "a form of homeostasis, the equilibration of opposed vested interests within a series of specialized interdependent functional systems."[11]

But despite the presence of theoretical statements such as these, when historians turn to the examination of na-

---

[11] Quand ceux qui possèdent, comme moi, des champs et des maisons, s'assemblent pour leurs intérêts communs, j'ai ma voix dans cette assemblée; je suise une partie du tout, une partie de la communauté, une partie de la souveraineté: voilà ma patrie." Voltaire, *Dictionnaire Philosophique,* under the entry, "Patrie"; Kohn, *Idea of Nationalism,* 17; Karl W. Deutsch *et al., Political Community and the North Atlantic Area* (Princeton, 1957), 55"; Shafer, *Nationalism* 100–105, 115; Louis L. Snyder, *The Meaning of Nationalism* (New Brunswick, N. J., 1954), 83. See also Curti, *The Roots of American Loyalty,* Chap. IV, "The Economics of Loyalty," 92–121, 161.

tionalism in specific cases, they often seem to neglect the factor of common interest, and to focus their attention very heavily upon common cultural factors. This neglect—curious in any case—has been all the more strange in view of the fact that an emphasis upon the importance of self-interest would fit in well with certain points which the historians customarily stress. One of these is the idea that modern nationalism has risen concurrently with modern democracy. Hans Kohn, for instance, regards this correlation as so close that he denies the existence of any fully developed nationalism prior to the French Revolution.[12] In this connection it is clear that the rise of democrary represents an admission of the masses to certain civic privileges and expectations of property ownership—that is, to a stake in society. The nation state, of course, served as the instrument for the protection of this stake, and the people's spirit of loyalty to the nation was partly their response to that which protected their interests. Until democracy gave them an interest to protect, they were incapable of this response—incapable of nationalism. Hector St. Jean de Crèvecoeur recognized this factor of self-interest very clearly in 1782, when he explained why European immigrants to America proved so quick to develop a loyalty to their new country:

What attachment can a poor European emigrant have for a country where he had nothing? The knowledge of a language, the love of a few kindred as poor as himself, were the only cords that tied him: his country is now that which gives him land, bread, protection, and consequence. *Ubi panis, ibi patria* is the motto of all emigrants.[13]

---
[12] Kohn, *The Idea of Nationalism*, 3, 10.
[13] Hector St. Jean de Crèvecoeur, *Letters from an American Farmer* (London, 1782, in Everyman's Library, New York, 1912), 41–44.

Another well-recognized aspect of nationalism, into which the factor of self-interest again fits clearly, is the invigorating effect which war has had upon national spirit. Heinrich von Treitschke reduced this to a simple and oft-repeated formula: "Again and again, it has been proved that it is war which turns a people into a nation." Frederick Hertz, who deplored the fact as much as Treitschke rejoiced in it, agreed: "War could be called the greatest instrument of national unification, but for the fact that it also fosters the growth of forces which often imply a new menace to national unity." [14]

How does war produce this effect? No doubt it does so in a variety of ways and by appealing to a variety of impulses, some of which are irrational. But certainly one of the effects of war is to reorient the pattern of conflicts of interest within any national population. In times of peace, the diversity of interests of various kinds tends to divide the people into antagonistic groups—what James Madison called factions and what we now call pressure groups—and these groups compete for control of public policy. Their relation to one another is primarily one of rivalry. Even in wartime these rivalries will continue; but they tend to become secondary, for war subjects all interests to a common danger and to more vital danger than they ever incur from one another. In the presence of such danger, all interests tend to work together. In this way, war harnesses the motives of self-interest, which ordinarily pull in various directions, and causes them all to pull in the same direction and thus to reinforce the spirit of nationalism.

Despite the importance of democracy as a means of enlarging the community of interest, despite the importance

---

[14] Frederick Hertz, *Nationality in History and Politics* (New York, 1944), 37, 218–19. Treitschke is quoted by Shafer, *Nationalism*, 45.

of war as a means of drawing interests which would otherwise be divisive into conjunction, and despite the close correlations which historians have drawn between nationalism on the one hand and democracy and war on the other, these same historians have, for the most part, still failed to follow the logic of their own arguments, and have continued to explain specific nationalistic movements in terms of culture. One has only to read Louis L. Snyder's exhaustive book-length review of the treatments of nationalism by historians, political scientists, economists, social psychologists, psychoanalysts and psychiatrists to perceive how constantly social scientists of all kinds have relied either upon cultural factors or upon social behavior that results from cultural factors as the master key to nationalism.

This commitment extends far. It controls the thinking of many historians so completely that whenever a population manifests nationalistic tendencies, the historian, by reflex, reaches for evidence of the growth of cultural bonds as the only conceivable means of explanation. Conversely, whenever deep cleavages appear in a previously nationalized group he hypothesizes the evolution of a separate, new culture as the basis of a new nationalism, and husbands every scrap of evidence, however tenuous, which lends itself to his hypothesis. Although he perhaps recognizes the importance of interests in the abstract, he almost never focuses upon them when analyzing a specific national movement.

To argue that the factor of common interests is an important and somewhat neglected element in nationalism, and that it ought to receive substantial attention, does not mean at all that the concept of interest should replace the concept of culture. The point is rather that nationalism rests on two psychological bases rather than one—feeling of common culture on the one hand and feeling of common interests on the other. It is questionable whether either basis can support a superstructure of nationality without the other. If the historian will recognize this dualism, he will not only possess an effective working concept, but will also free himself from his present compulsion to prove a growth of cultural unity every time he observes an intensification of nationalism and to prove the emergence of a new culture every time a dissident group proclaims its solidarity in nationalistic terms.

Here, then, are a number of propositions about the historian's treatment of nationalism: that he conceives of it abstractly, in sound theoretical terms, regarding it as a form of group loyalty psychologically similar to other forms of group loyalty, and having the subjective, relativistic, developmental qualities which other forms of group loyalty possess; that the close relation between nationalism and the political state warps the historian's view and causes him to treat it functionally as a monolithic form of loyalty, in antithesis to other forms of group loyalty, instead of recognizing that it is associated with and even derived from those other loyalties; that his use of the concept as a sanction to validate the demands of some groups for autonomy, while denying the similar demands of other groups, leads him into a fallacious correlation between the ethical rightness of a group's policies and the objective separateness of the group's identity; that this valuative use of the concept also impels him to explain the origins of nationalism in terms of deep-seated, long-enduring natural affinities among a people, or in other words to rely too heavily upon cultural factors in his explanation even where they are tenuous; that this cultural emphasis has, in turn, caused him frequently to overlook factors of self-interest, which have been vital in many historic situations in the integration or in the disintegration of national loyalties.

If these general propositions have any validity, it should be possible to test them by applying them to specific historical situations. Any reader of this paper will perhaps test them in terms of the historical treatment of the nationality or national movement with which he himself is most familiar. For myself, they can most readily be applied in the field of American history. The rest of this paper, therefore, is devoted to a consideration of their applicability at that point in American history where the question of nationalism is most critical and most complex—namely in the crisis leading to the Civil War.

It is a truism that because of the vast extent of the United States and its great physiographic variety, major areas within the Union have often found their interests in conflict, and the alignment on public issues has followed geographical lines far more often than would occur in a smaller or more homogeneous country. These geographically aligned differentials have, in fact, been a pervasive factor and have presented themselves in many different forms. At times, such as the period of Jacksonian democracy or the Populist revolt, the divisions between East and West have seemed more fundamental than those between North and South, and careful analysis has always shown that these regional differentiations extended beyond a mere dualism. The West, with its frontier attributes, played a distinctive role even during the period when North-South antagonisms were most acute, and indeed the struggle which came to a crisis in 1861 has been seen by Frederick Jackson Turner to consist of a rivalry between the North and the South to draw the West into their respective orbits. Even while North and South were approaching the climactic rivalry of the Civil War, internal conflicts also made themselves felt at a different level, as issues arose between industrial and agricultural areas within the North, or between plantation belts and backwoods districts within the South.

Historians speak of these areas in which distinctive groups are localized or concentrated as sections, and they recognize sectionalism (the tension between such areas) as one of the major themes of American history. In most cases of sectional rivalry, the question of nationalism has not been involved, for the people of one sectional area have not called into question the Union which they share with the rival section, and the loyalties which they give to their own area have not impinged directly upon their national loyalty to the Union. Even when sectional bitterness reached the emotional pitch which it developed in 1896 the rivals sought only to impose their policies upon one another within the Union, not to sever their ties with one another by disrupting the Union.

In the era between 1848 and 1861, however, America's geographically aligned rivalries were drawn into a pattern of intense conflict between the North and the South, and the group loyalties of the people in the South were focused upon a Southern republic in a way which undercut the American nationalism that had previously focused upon the Union. In this case, then, Southernism, instead of working sectionally within a framework of nationalism, tended to take on the character of nationalism itself and to break down the existing pattern of nationalism. Since the Southern movement began as a sectional reaction against this existing pattern, historians frequently evaluate the conflict which developed in terms of sectionalism *versus* nationalism.

In strict logic the antithesis of sectionalism *versus* nationalism would not necessarily link one region (the South with sectionalism, or the other region (the North) with nationalism. On the contrary, it might be argued that nationalistic forces in both the North and the South which placed the welfare of the Union above all regional values were pitted against sectional forces in both regions which gave primary values to regional objectives—such as, for the South, the protection of slavery in the territories or, for the North, the exclusion of slavery from the territories. Viewed in this way, the conflict might be said to involve the triumph of sectionalism over American nationalism within both regions and an ensuing conflict between Northern sectionalism and Southern sectionalism. Alternatively, it might also be argued that Northern group loyalty of the most fundamental kind found a focus in the Union formed in 1787, while Southern group loyalty, also of the deepest sort, found a new focus in a separate Southern republic. Regarded in this way, the conflict might be construed as, in fact, many historians do construe it—as a conflict between Northern (Union) nationalism and Southern (Confederate) nationalism.

Either of these formulations has a certain tenability in theory. In operative terms, however, the forces which saved the American Union were of course centered in the North and those which sought to disrupt it were centered in the South. Consequently it seemed natural afterward, in light of the Union's survival, to link each of the forces at work with one of the rival regions and to speak of nationalism as Northern and sectionalism as Southern.

This attribution, however, at once has the effect of bringing the valuative aspect of the concept of nationalism into play. It clearly implies a sanction for the Northern position—the sanction that the "people" involved in the crisis were the American people, both North and South, since the Union was the nation, whereas those in the South who "felt themselves to be one" were not one in the ultimate sense, since the impulse which prompted their unity was sectional rather than national. Of course, insofar as hindsight furnishes a legitimate criterion, the conclusion, if not the reason, was valid, for what the North defended has found fulfillment as a nation and what the South defended has not. But the questionable feature of this reasoning is that it moves completely away from the psychological or functional aspects of nationalism toward an analysis that is almost entirely institutional. It has the effect of prejudging the question which is purportedly under examination, settling by ascription a point which ought to be settled by the evaluation of evidence. Instead of testing the validity of Union and Confederacy as nations by examining the character of the group loyalties attached to them, it bases a judgment of those group loyalties upon a prior assumption concerning the character, respectively of the Union and the Confederacy. By a trick of semantics it makes the question of group loyalties irrelevant, the assumption being that no matter what degree of cohesion or intensity these loyalties may have attained, they are not "national" unless they attach to a national institution. But the national insitution is the result simply of success in fulfilling national impulses, and to say that the Southern impulse was not nationalism because it did not in the long run maintain its attempted institutional form (the Southern Confederacy) is simply to say that it was not nationalism because it was not successful. Here one is reminded of the old riddle, Why is treason never successful? Answer: Because if it is successful it is not treason. In fact, the answer has a kind of truth, for treason, as a legal offense, has to be institutionally defined. But nationalism should not be treated in such institutional terms.

I have already suggested that the element of sanction in the institutional concept sometimes makes it difficult for the historian to attribute nationality to movements of which he morally disapproves, since the attribution itself would imply that the movement has a kind of validity. This factor has certainly influenced the treatment of the question whether the Southern Confederacy was a nation, for the issue between the Union and the Confederacy also became an issue between freedom and slavery. To ascribe nationality to the South is to validate the right of a proslavery movement to autonomy and self-determination. Since few historians in the twentieth century have been willing to do this, their moral position has sometimes run counter to their theory of nationality and has impelled them to shirk the consequences of their own belief that group identity is the basis for autonomy. In other words, once the ethical question of the character of Southern institutions becomes linked with the factual question of the nature of the group loyalties in the South, it becomes very difficult for the historian to deal with the factual question purely on its own merits. If the finding that a majority of Southern citizens wanted a nation of their own is inseparable from the conclusion that the institution of slavery enjoyed a democratic sanction, it is always possible to reverse the reasoning and to argue that since slavery could not have enjoyed a democratic sanction, therefore the Southern people must not have been a "people" in the sense that would entitle them to want a nation of their own.

The position of the strongly antislavery historian on the question of Southern nationality tends to be particularly ironic, for he usually emphasizes more than do most writers the depth of the division between the North and the South. No one stresses more than he the profound authoritarian implications of slavery for the entire intellectual and social life of the South, and the sharpness of the contrast between this society, with its system of legalized caste status, and the free, democratic society of the North. Yet, after making this case, the antislavery historian often takes the view that the Southern assertion of nationality was not justified. Of course, he might simply follow the logic of his moral position and argue that war is justified if waged by one nation to compel another nation to give up slavery. But since he also attaches moral value to the right of self-determination, the recognition of Southern nationality would place him in a moral dilemma. The only way he can have his crusade against slavery and his right of self-determination too is to deny that the principle of self-determination is involved in the case of the crusade against slavery, or in short to deny that the slaveholding belligerent was endowed with such nationality as his own analysis has pretty well demonstrated.

This statement, it might be added, is not intended to deny or question the primacy of moral considerations. It may well be that the abolition of slavery is worth more to mankind than the right of self-determination of peoples, especially since slavery itself denies this right to the slaves. Even if coercion is an evil, it may not be the worst of evils, and a war of subjugation may well be justified by the emancipation of 3,950,000 slaves. It may also be, as Lincoln apparently believed, that the preservation, even by force, of the union which had been formalized by the Constitution of 1787 has a higher value than the purely voluntary self-determination of peoples. All I mean to argue is that a historian should not assert that he regards the right of self-determination as an absolute and then argue that it is not involved in cases where he is unwilling to apply it, or where he thinks some other value has a higher priority.

The equation of Northernism with nationalism and Southernism with sectionalism not only denies by prejudgment, and without actual analysis of group feelings, that the Southern movement could have been national; it also leads to an easy assumption that all Northern support for federal authority must have been nationalistic rather than sectional. But this view tends to obscure the fact that in the North as well as in the South there were deep sectional impulses, and support or nonsupport of the Union was sometimes a matter of sectional tactics rather than of national loyalty. For instance, Northern support for a sectional tariff or for sectional internal improvements, adopted by sectional majorities in the national government, was no less sectional than Southern opposition to them. Northern efforts to put the terminus of a Pacific railroad at Chicago were no less sectional than Southern efforts to put it at New Orleans. Northern determination to keep Negroes (rather than just slaves) out of the territories was no less sectional than Southern determination to carry them there. Even Northern support for Lincoln, who did not so much as run in most of the slave states in 1860, was perhaps just as sectional as Southern support for Breckenridge or for Bell, who did not carry a single free state.

But in the North, sectional forces tended to support a strong Union because it was evident that this Union was becoming one in which the sectional forces of the North would be dominant. Thus the national Union could be made the instrument of these sectional interests. The South, on the other hand, finding itself in a minority position, could not hope to secure national support for sectional objectives, nor even to keep sectional and national interests in coordination with one another, and therefore it was forced to choose between section and nation. If the proslavery elements seemed less nationalistic than the antislavery elements, it was not because one more than the other put peace or national harmony above the question of slavery—for neither of them did—but because the antislavery elements could expect, with their majority status, to employ the national authority for their purposes, while the proslavery forces could not. A Northerner could, and many Northerners did, support the Union for sectional reasons;[15] no Southerner was likely to support it for any other than national reasons.

The historian certainly should make some distinction between the nationalistic motive to support the Union as the embodiment of the "people" as a whole, and the tactical motive to use the authority of the Union for the promotion of sectional interests; but very often both of these impulses are called by the same name, i.e. nationalism.

If the antithesis of Northern nationalism and Southern sectionalism conceals the sectional motivation of much that was done through national means in the North, it also obscures another important reality: namely that a mixture of regional and national loyalties prevailed on both sides. These mixed loyalties did not seem ambiguous or inconsistent in the North because they were not in conflict there, whereas in the South they did conflict and, because they did, were made to seem evidence of what amounted to duplicity—as if devotion to the section in itself demonstrated alienation from the nation and as if nationalism could flourish only as regional loyalties withered away. But

---

[15] Curti (*Roots of American Loyalty,* 111) says, "Webster cleverly associated national interest with all the policies which his opponents declared to be sectional in character—tariffs, internal improvements . . . and restriction of the disposal of public lands in the West."

in fact, this view is mistaken. To take one concrete example, there was no equivocation on the part of Josiah Quincy of Massachusetts when he declared in 1811 that "the first public love of my heart is the Commonwealth of Massachusetts . . . the love of this Union grows out of this attachment to my native soil." Nor was there ambiguity in Sam Houston of Texas when he asserted that he was a Southerner and a Unionist too, with "a Southern heart, large enough, I trust, to embrace the whole Union if not the whole world"; nor in J. B. D. De Bow when he appealed to his fellow-citizens, "as Southerners, as *Americans,* as MEN"; nor in Alexander H. Stephens of Georgia when he said, "I have a patriotism that embraces, I trust, all parts of the Union, . . . yet I must confess my feelings of attachment are most ardent toward that with which all my interests and associations are identified. . . . The South is my home, my fatherland." [16]

If the point here were only that the people of the South became trapped in a conflict of loyalties, it would hardly be worth stating; historians have known it as a truism for a long time. The point is rather that the Northerners and the Southerners were not distinguished from one another by a singularity of loyalty on one side and a multiplicity of loyalties on the others, as though one had been monogamous and the other polygamous. In fact, they both had multiple loyalties, and what distinguished them was that one, being in a majority, was able to keep all its loyalties

---

[16] Josiah Quincy, in *Annals of Congress,* 11th Cong., 3rd sess., col. 542 (Jan. 14, 1811); Sam Houston, in *Congressional Globe,* 31st Cong., 1st sess., Appendix, 102 (Feb. 8, 1850); J. D. B. De Bow in *De Bow's Review,* III (May 1847), 421, quoted in Robert F. Durden, "J. D. B. De Bow: Convolutions of a Slavery Expansionist," *Journal of Southern History,* XVII (Nov. 1951), 445; Alexander H. Stephens, in *Congressional Globe,* 28th Cong., 2nd sess., Appendix, 313–14, (Jan. 25, 1845).

coordinated, and therefore undivided, while the other, being in a minority, was not able to keep them coordinated, with the result that they did become divided. Multiple loyalties do not inherently produce conflict, and the question whether conflict will develop is entirely separate from the question whether loyalties are multiple.

It would be misleading in the extreme, however, to suggest that the valuative implication of the concept of nationalism has warped only the views of writers whose sympathies lie with the Union. For if it has led some of them to deny that the South was entitled to the sanction of nationality, and to make this denial with little or no reference to psychological realities, it has also led some writers whose sympathies lie with the South to assert that the Southern claim to nationhood was validated by a complete cultural separateness, and to make this assertion with equally small reference to the cultural realities.

This is not to deny that there was distinctiveness in the Southern culture. Southern conservatism, Southern hierarchy, the cult of chivalry, the unmachined civilization, the folk society, the rural character of the life, the clan values rather than the commercial values—all had a deeply significant distinctiveness. But this is not quite the same as *separateness,* and the efforts of historians to buttress their claim that the South had a wholly separate culture, self-consciously asserting itself as a cultural counterpart of political nationalism, have led, on the whole, to paltry results. Southern writers, like the nationalistic fabricators of culture mentioned above, issued periodic manifestoes proclaiming that the South should have its own literature, but their efforts failed for lack of support from Southern readers. Southern educators likewise deplored the infiltration of Yankee ideas in the schools, and when the crisis was most acute, Southern students departed with great fanfare from Northern colleges. But Southern education continued to be American education. In the economic area, a few Southern fire-eaters made a conspicuous point of the fact that they were wearing homespun, proclaiming the need for a Southern economic self-sufficiency which was never realized. But it is crucial that the advocates of a Southern culture spent much of their time complaining that the South would not accept their cultural program. Evidence of this kind is a tenuous basis indeed for arguing that Southern nationalism sprang from a full-bodied Southern culture.[17] If historians had not been captives to the idea that nationality equates with culture, and that where there is separate nationalism there must be culture of equivalent separateness, they would probably have been far quicker to recognize how very thin the historical evidences of a separate Southern culture really are. They would also have been disposed to give more emphasis to the many important cultural features which Southerners shared with other nineteenth-century Americans: the common language which was a transatlantic modification of

---

[17] Important studies of cultural aspects of southern nationalism are: Jay Hubbell, "Literary Nationalism in the Old South," in *American Studies in Honor of William K. Boyd*, ed. D. K. Jackson (Durham, N. C., 1940); John S. Ezell, "A Southern Education for Southrons," *Journal of Southern History*, XVII (Aug. 1951), 303–27; Merle Curti, *The Growth of American Thought* (New York, 1943), Chap. XVII; Curtis Carroll Davis, *Chronicler of the Cavaliers: A Life of the Virginia Novelist, Dr. William A. Caruthers* (Richmond, 1953); Rollin G. Osterweis, *Romanticism and Nationalism in the Old South* (New Haven, 1949); Avery O. Craven, *The Growth of Southern Nationalism, 1848–1861* (Baton Rouge, 1953). Despite voluminous data, however, these studies lend themselves to the argument that a great effort was being made to create a sense of cultural separateness by self-conscious means, where it scarcely existed objectively. An unpublished paper by Stanley Bailis, written in my graduate seminar at Yale in 1958–1959, developed this point very forcibly and effectively.

English, much the same in both the North and the South; the common religion of a people who were overwhelmingly evangelical and Protestant as well as Christian; the common political commitment to democratic institutions; the common system of values which exalted progress, material success, individual self-reliance, and distrust of authority; and the bumptious Americanism which scorned the "decadent monarchies" of the Old World.[18]

But some historians have been compulsively impelled to minimize these factors and to assert the existence of a separate Southern culture, just as others have been compulsively impelled to deny that the Southern movement represented a full nationalism. Just as the antislavery sympathizer finds that his view of the degree of Southern nationalism cannot be formed on the merits of the question without reference to his conviction that the South had no right to thwart the forces working toward emancipation, so the Southern sympathizer finds that his view of the separateness of Southern culture cannot be formed on the merits of the question without reference to his conviction that the South enjoyed a full national identity, which finds its ultimate sanction in the possession of a full-fledged culture. The attribution of culture is evaluative for the question of nationality, just as the question of nationality, in turn, is evaluate for the justification of the acts of a group claiming a right to exercise autonomy.

To appreciate one important reason for the emphasis of modern historians upon the separateness of the Southern culture, it is necessary only to look at the difference in the

---

[18] Hans Kohn, *American Nationalism: An Interpretative Essay* (New York, 1957), 106–21, demonstrates far better than most historians of the South the ambivalence in both the cultural affiliations and the loyalties of the people of the South on the eve of the Civil War.

way in which the defense of the South has been argued in the more remote and in the more recent past. From the Civil War until 1900, it was notorious that no Southerner seemed capable of writing on any aspect of the Civil War without including a lengthy disquisition on the legal and constitutional right of secession, with copious attention to the exact contractual understandings reached in 1787. But no historian has elaborated such arguments now for more than a generation. Why? Certainly not because the South no longer has defenders. The answer, I think, is that nowadays we do not couch our historical defenses in formalistic or legalistic terms. The sanction for what the South did in 1861 is no longer believed to be what it had agreed to in 1787. The sanction depends rather upon what the Southerners were in 1861—whether they constituted a people in the sense which entitled them to exercise what we now call autonomy or self-determination, rather than what we used to call sovereignty. But insofar as the same conclusion is reached as to whether the South was justified, and insofar as the reasons ostensibly leading to the conclusion may be in fact derived from the conclusion instead of the conclusion being derived from them, the great transformation since the nineteenth century from formalism to functionalism has perhaps not increased the realism of our thinking as much as we sometimes fondly imagine.

The significance of this subtle relation between descriptive observations and their valuative implications is not that it results in specious reasoning, from conclusion to premise instead of from premise to conclusion. It is rather that it tends to reduce the whole analysis to a set of oversimplified antitheses or polarities whose greatest fault is not that they are partisan, but simply that they do not explain anything.

If North and South fought; if one was a "nation" and

one was not; if the people of one were "loyal" and those of the other were "disloyal"; or, on the other hand, if they constituted two diverse civilizations, then the investigator is under strong compulsion to reduce the complex forces of the 1850's to simplicity and to come up with antitheses which will fit these dualisms. Hence, we have had a series of sweeping and dramatic contrasts which present North and South in polar terms. Indeed the historiography of the subject is largely a record of how one pair of alternatives has been set up, only to be knocked down and replaced by another.

Thus we were once told that the South was a land of Cavaliers, the North, an abode of Puritans; or that the South stood for states' rights, while North stood for the federal supremacy. Later historians rejected these formulae as fallacious or superficial,[19] but the old yearning for a sharp, clear-cut antithesis still shaped historical thought, and two other, more formidable dualisms were advanced. One of these was primarily an economic argument, brilliantly set forth by Charles A. Beard, that Southern agrarianism and Northern industrialism must necessarily clash because of their dissimilarity. The other was the more broadly social view that North and South were, in fact, "diverse civilizations," and as such, incapable of maintaining a union with one another.[20]

The quest for an unqualified antithesis still continues.

---

[19] The "Puritan *versus* Cavalier" thesis began to fade in 1910, when Thomas J. Wertenbaker published *Patrician and Plebeian in Virginia* (Charlottesville, Va., 1910); the formalistic weakness of the concept of states' rights *versus* nationalism was demonstrated by Arthur M. Schlesinger in "The State Rights Fetish," in *New Viewpoints in American History* (New York, 1922).

[20] Charles A. and Mary R. Beard, *The Rise of American Civilization* (2 vols., New York, 1927). One of the authoritative spokesmen of the idea of diverse civilizations was Edward Channing, in his *History of the United States* (6 vols., New York, 1905–1925; VI, 3–4).

Interpretations now current have turned back to an emphasis, formerly popular in the nineteenth century, upon the basic incompatibility between a slaveholding and a non-slaveholding regime, with all the far-reaching differences in social values and in mode of life which such systems must entail.[21]

These antitheses are in a sense caricatures, perhaps accurate in singling out some distinctive feature, but grossly distorted in the emphasis which they give to it. Because of their vulnerability, revisionist critics have been able to direct damaging criticism at every one of them. The fervently evangelical South, with a large infusion of frontier primitivism and equalitarianism, was by no means Cavalier, while the Puritanism which may have dominated New England but had certainly never dominated the North as a whole, was already beginning to be diluted by immigration and urbanization at least two decades before the Civil War. Moreover, there were no fully articulated "planter" and "industrial" civilizations, standing in juxtaposition to one another, for the common conditions of life of plain farmers throughout an overwhelmingly rural republic completely transcended these distinctions. Dirt farmers, south and north, were the backbone of both sections, planter aristocrats and rising industrialists notwithstanding.[22]

---

[21] Arthur Schlesinger, Jr., in "The Causes of the Civil War: A Note on Historical Sentimentalism," *Partisan Review*, XVI (Oct. 1949), 469–81; and Harry V. Jaffa, in *Crisis of the House Divided: An Interpretation of the Issues in the Lincoln-Douglas Debates* (New York, 1959), have done much to reinstate the idea that the conflict was a struggle between freedom and slavery, but Leon F. Litwack, *North of Slavery: The Negro in the Free States, 1790–1860* (Chicago, 1961), shows that even a genuine sectional division on the slavery question did not necessarily mean any great sectional discrepancy in attitudes toward the Negro. Racism was nationwide.

[22] James G. Randall in "The Civil War Restudied," *Journal of Southern History*, VI (Nov. 1940), 439–57, exposed some of the fallacies in the views that agrarian and industrial societies were certain to clash, and that North and South formed diametrically opposed civilizations.

Similarly, the political and economic antitheses contain fallacies. Shrewd observers have always perceived the states' rights doctrine to be less a philosophical position than a tactical device, attractive to any minority regardless of latitude, and the doctrine of national supremacy to be one exalted by those who possessed power and wanted to take advantage of it. Scratch a spokesman of state sovereignty and you find, not necessarily a Southerner, but almost invariably a man who sees that he is outnumbered; look beneath the rhetoric which exalts federal supremacy and you discover a motive on the part of a majority group to remove some irksome restriction upon the use of power.

The once-regnant theory that the Civil War was a "clash of economic sections," and that agriculture and industry must inevitably conflict was hardly less than an assumption that where economies are diversified, they must invariably be antagonistic. There were, in fact, serious antagonisms between the cotton economy and the manufacturing interest, but the trouble with making a theory of them is that it will lead logically to the conclusion that no country can ever achieve real integration economically: although a country without economic diversity would find its integrity as a nation threatened because it is not self-sufficient, if it were to attain economic diversity, it would theoretically find its integrity as a nation threatened because diverse interests had led to internal dissensions. The assumption in the first instance is that diverse interests will be complementary; in the second instance, that they will be incompatible. Both are merely assumptions, valid or not according to the individual circumstances; there are many situations in which agricultural areas and industrial areas serve each other as sources of supplies and as markets. Such complementary situations show the fallacy in the *a priori* supposition that points of dissimilarity are equivalent to points of dissension.

Compared to these other dualisms, the antithesis between slaveholding and non-slaveholding states is at least valid in that there were in fact two groups of states sharply differentiated in the legal status they gave to slavery. This distinction was clear-cut and uncontrovertible, as was not the case with the other dualisms that have been mentioned. But even here, the antitheses is less deep than might be supposed, for the distinction was not between one society which accorded equality to the Negro and another which denied it; in fact racism was nationwide, and neither Abraham Lincoln nor any other major leader proposed to place the Negro on the same basis with other citizens. The issue as it stood at that time, unfortunately, was less a question whether the Negro should have status as an equal than a dispute over what form his inferior status should take. For the Negro in America, chattel servitude was sectional but caste inferiority was still national, and thus the slavery issue also failed to present a complete contrast.

Even the seemingly manifest difference between the loyalties of a nationalistic North and a sectionalistic South becomes tenuous when it is examined closely. For copious evidence shows that national as well as local loyalties prevailed in both the North and the South. The North's so-called "nationalism," consisted as I have already pointed out, partly in its control over federal policy, and in the ability to keep it in alignment with sectional interests, while the South's "sectionalism" was, at least initially an expression of the lack of such a capacity.

The problem presented by such antitheses as these in the interpretation of history, however, arises not from their oversimplifications or their exaggeration of differences, but from their mistaken attribution of mutual exclusiveness to phenomena which naturally coexist and overlap as national identity and regional identity do. It is false to assume that nationalism is a matter of homogeneity and therefore to conclude that regional diversity—at least when it appears on a North-South axis—is inconsistent with national unity. Once the mistaken assumption of mutual exclusiveness is accepted, the false conclusion follows that sectional distinctiveness can serve as an index of deviation, and by the same token that loyalty to the section can become an index of disloyalty to the Union. Beside mistaking dissimilarity for antagonism, this kind of interpretation has the tendency, where friction exists, to shift attention away from specific disputes between parties and to emphasize their mere lack of resemblance to one another.

The habit of equating diversity with dissension, and of using the word "difference" to mean both at the same time, has taken such deep root in the historiography of the Civil War that it becomes difficult to dissociate the two; nevertheless, history abounds in instances where diversity does not lead to antagonism, where regional identity does not detract from national integrity, and where no one expects them to do so. Outside the United States, for instance, the French, Catholic, peasant culture of the Quebec province presents sharper contrasts to the English, Protestant, pioneer culture of Ontario than North and South ever presented, and strong elements of antagonism have been involved historically; yet there was no "irrepressible conflict" in Canada, and today the diversity is hardly regarded as a serious problem. Within the United States, New Englanders, with their Puritan heritage and their Yankee ways, have kept their distinctiveness, along with a strong affection for their "stern and rockbound coast"; yet these qualities are regarded as reinforcing rather than diminishing the

Yankee's Americanism. Even where the South itself is involved, historical interpretation of sectional differences has been too inconsistent to bear scrutiny. From the ratification of the Constitution until the high noon of the New Deal, and to some extent even down to the present, the South has been set apart by its rural society, its staple-crop economy, its tradition of leadership or control by the landowning interest, its large proportion of Negro population and its formalized system of caste in race relations. In 1787 these differences were perhaps more pronounced than during the crisis which led to the Civil War, yet historians who assume that such regional dissimilarities made a continuation of peaceful union impossible after 1850 seem completely untroubled by the fact that the very same diversities did not at all prevent the formation of at least a loose union in 1787–1788, or the rapid and triumphant growth of American nationalism for nearly forty years thereafter. Since the Civil War, the one-party system of the "solid" South, and the relative poverty of the region, as well as the heritage of bitterness from Civil War and Reconstruction, have made the sectional contrasts in some respects sharper than they were during the antebellum period. Yet these strong sectional factors proved not inconsistent with the swift restoration of American nationalism in the South, which increased steadily at least until 1954.[23] The sectional differences were still there, but in this new context, since they did not lead to war, no one supposed any longer that they must be inherently disruptive. In fact, the readiness with which the South returned to the Union will defy explanation unless

---

[23] Paul H. Buck, *The Road to Reunion, 1865–1900* (Boston, 1937), traces a swift and easy restoration of harmony between North and South within thirty-five years of Appomattox, which could not possibly have occurred if Southern nationalism had been so deep-seated as, for instance, Polish nationalism was.

it is recognized that Southern loyalties to the Union were never really obliterated but rather were eclipsed by other loyalties with which, for a time, they conflicted. It was a dim awareness of this among the participants in the Civil War which gave the conflict its peculiarly tragic tone—its pathos as a "brothers' war."

The historian may feel acutely the need for an explanation of the deep alienation which developed between North and South in the middle of the nineteenth century, but he ought not to allow the urgency of this need to blind him to the fact that he also needs an explanation for the growth of American nationalism between 1800 and 1846 and for the smoothness of the "road to reunion" between 1865 and 1900. No explanation of the sectional strife is really much good if it makes these phenomena of harmony and reconciliation appear impossible. Yet the historian's reliance upon the sharpest conceivable antitheses has led him to explain the schism in terms so deep and total that the subsequent readiness of Southern men, in 1898 and 1917, to enlist in the United States Army and to fight under the American flag would seem quite incredible.

To explain an antagonism which sprang up suddenly, and died down suddenly, the historian does not need to discover, and cannot effectively use, a factor which has been constant over a long period, as the cultural difference between the North and the South has been. He needs to identify a factor which can cause bitter disagreement even among a people who have much basic homogeneity. No factor, I would suggest, will meet this need better than the feeling, widespread in the 1850's in the South that the South's vital interests were being jeopardized, and that the region was being exposed to the dangers of a slave insurrection, as a result of the hostility of antislavery men in the North. Applied to the sectional crisis, such a view of the sources of friction would make possible the explanation of the Civil War, without making impossible the explanation of the rapid return to union after the war. No cultural explanation will do this.

The cultural factor and the factor of self-interest are, of course, not wholly unrelated, for essential interests are determined partly by cultural values and *vice versa*. But the fact remains that within an integrated culture acute conflicts of interest may be generated, and between diverse cultures strong community of interests may develop. A body of citizens may exalt the national state as the instrument that unites them with those with whom they have an affinity, but they may also exalt it as the guardian of certain essential interests and social values which they do not necessarily share with the over-all society. Despite the emphasis in historical literature upon cultural homogeneity, history itself offers extensive evidence that if a state protects the interests—either real or fancied—of culturally disparate groups in its population, it can command the nationalistic loyalty of such groups without reducing them to a homogeneous body of citizens, and that if it systematically disregards the interests of a group it alienates the group and makes cultural affinities with the majority seem irrelevant.[24] The state, of course, frequently adopts measures adverse to

---

[24] Grodzins (*The Loyal and the Disloyal*, ii) quotes George Washington: "Men . . . may talk of patriotism . . . but whoever builds upon it as the basis for conducting a long and bloody war will find themselves deceived in the end. We must take the passions of men as nature has given them, and those principles as a guide which are generally the rule of Action. I do not mean to exclude altogether the Idea of Patriotism. I know it exists, and I know it has done much in the present Contest. But I will venture to assert, that a great and lasting war can never be supported on this principle alone. It must be aided by a prospect of Interest or some reward."

the specific advantage of a given group without seriously endangering the basis of their loyalty, but when it acts against what the group conceives to be its fundamental welfare, there is a question whether loyalty can survive. In fact the members of a group may become alienated even more readily when they feel that they have been victimized by their own kindred rather than by strangers. In this sense, community of interest may sometimes be a more important condition for nationalism than cultural homogeneity, and conflict of interest may be a greater danger to national union than cultural diversity.

Without laboring this point, it may be worth noting that in situations where conflict occurs, cultural diversity is never the direct cause. This diversity will generate friction only when it has been translated into opposing policies for dealing with a particular question. Therefore even the historian who relies entirely upon cultural explanations to account for a given conflict must reckon with the fact that the disruptive potentials inherent in cultural diversity remain latent until conflicts of interest bring them into play.

Insofar as it is sound to regard the equilibration of interests as a condition necessary to nationalism, it follows that the American Civil War must be interpreted less in terms of antitheses and dissimilarities between North and South, and more in terms of the prolonged sequence of interest-conflicts which crystallized along sectional lines. Southerners became progressively more alienated as they became more convinced, first, that the Union was sacrificing their economic welfare by its tariff policy; later, that it was denying them parity in the process of national expansion; and finally that it was condoning the activities of men who would loose a slave insurrection upon them and expose them to possible butchery.

This does not mean, of course, that anyone need turn to a simple economic interpretation of history, but rather that we should recognize that cultural similarities alone will not provide a basis of affinity between groups who regard each others' policies as endangering their own security. The danger of these conflicts to national unity was fully recognized as early as 1797 and was a major theme in Washington's Farewell Address. Later, control of the national political system became itself a weapon in the warfare between opposing interests, and as it did so, the central government lost much of its potency as a symbol evocative of national loyalties.

Whether slavery did or did not constitute a vital interest for the South is too large a question to be explored here, but there is no doubt that the South believed it did. Also there is no doubt that the emancipation of the slaves was the largest expropriation of property that has ever occurred in the United States—the heaviest blow that any large interest group has ever sustained. The slavery question was a thoroughly tangible matter, and far more than a symbol in a conflict of cultures, but many historians prefer to treat it as if it were no such thing. Southern writers have never wished to believe that the South fought for slavery, while Northern writers have preferred to think in terms of the fulfillment of an ideal of freedom rather than the overthrow of a vast property interest.

By focusing upon conflict of interest as a basic factor it is possible to explain the otherwise stubborn anomaly that the sectional crisis grew in intensity even as the republic grew in homogeneity. Originally, cultural unity was not deemed necessary to the welfare of the Union under the Constitution, and both the Northern and the Southern states fully intended to preserve their respective sectional peculiarities, of which they were acutely aware when they ratified the Constitution. Indeed, they did not ratify it until shrewd calculation had assured each section either that it might hope to gain preponderant weight, or at least that it would be strong enough to maintain the sectional equilibrium in the new system. If the republic had remained static, with the area and population of 1790 more or less permanent, an equilibrium might have been maintained, and the Union might have enjoyed harmony, even without homogeneity. The "house divided," which had in fact been divided from the beginning, might have continued to stand as it had stood for seventy years.

But when growth ensued—with uneven rates of advance for the two sections—the equilibrium was upset. The minority section lost its ability to exercise a joint control in the federal government, and with this control went the power of coordinating national with sectional objectives and thus of maintaining the image of the federal government as the guardian of the essential interests or values of Southern society. The South, therefore, was forced more and more to regard national objectives on the one hand and sectional objectives on the other as the alternatives of a painful choice. Meanwhile, the North did not have to choose between national and sectional objectives because by use of its power it could incorporate sectional goals into the national program. What was good for the North was good for the country, and thus no problem of priority need arise. The potential dilemma of Josiah Quincy's loyalties, which he had stated so clearly, remained a latent dilemma, never developed beyond the verbal level. But Sam Houston and Alexander Stephens lived to see a situation where bigness of heart was not enough and where the Union was so divided that patriotism could no longer embrace it.

If the adjustment of conflicting interests rather than the elimination of cultural differences is in this instance the key to the perpetuation of national unity, and if an equilibrium of power is the condition most favorable to the adjustment of conflicting interests, then the historian has an explanation for the seeming paradox that the crisis of American nationalism came not when regional diversity was greatest, but after many common denominators between the sections had developed and had substantially increased the measure of cultural uniformity. He has also a key to the anomalous fact that from 1787 to 1861, national growth always seemed to endanger national unity: it upset the equation between North and South by introducing new factors of power which potentially jeopardized sectional interests that had previously seemed to be in balance.

If the pattern of loyalties in America between 1820 and 1860 was more intricate than the stark antithesis of nationalism and sectionalism would imply, and if the ultimate conflict between North and South was in part the consequence of the failure of the Union to solve the problems of chronic conflict of interest, even after it had successfully begun to transcend the presumably more difficult obstacles of cultural dissimilarity, the implication is not that a new single-factor analysis should be applied, developing a view which presents the Civil War in the exclusive terms of a conflict between culturally similar groups which both spelled their version of nationalism with the alphabet of self-interest. It is rather to suggest that the valuative elements in the concept of nationalism have influenced too many of the findings of the historian, that the concept has warped his analysis as much as it has assisted it, and that the historical process is far too intricate to be handled in terms of the simple dualisms of culture *versus* culture, nation *versus* section, interest *versus* interest, or Americanism *versus* Southernism.

Millennia

Albert Léon Guérard

Albert Léon Guérard (1880–1959) describes in Personal Equation *his Paris childhood, his studies in England and his emigration to the United States. The great formative experience of his youth was the Dreyfus crisis, which had much to do with his lifelong liberal commitments: his socialist and internationalist faiths; his distrust of nationalism, "realism" and power politics; his antagonism to religious bigotries, to materialist complacency and to elites in general. He had intended to teach English literature in France, where he took his agrégation in English (first place) in 1906; however, in that year he went instead to the United States, where he married Wilhelmina McCartney in 1907. Up until 1925, he taught French literature and civilization, first at Williams College, then successively at Stanford University, Rice Institute and the University of California at Los Angles. In 1925 he returned to Stanford as Professor of General Literature in the Department of English, and created new courses in comparative literature and in literary criticism and theory. Nine of his books were published after his retirement from Stanford in 1946, and he was Professor of Comparative Literature at Brandeis University from 1950 to 1953. He had been naturalized in 1916, and served with the United States Army in the First World War and with the Office of War Information in the Second World War. He was a member of the National Institute of Letters.*

Guérard's diverse interests were expressed in twenty-six

books, twenty-three in English and three in French. The largest body of work consisted of twelve books in French history and civilization—from French Prophets of Yesterday *down to* France: A Modern History. Reflections on the Napoleonic Legend, The Life and Death of an Ideal, *the second volume of his work,* French Civilization, Napoleon III, *the first of two biographies on the subject,* Napoleon I *and* France: A Short History *received particular attention. The shift in mid-career to general literature led to four volumes of literary criticism and theory, of which* Preface to World Literature *is perhaps best known. Four volumes of spiritual autobiography evoke the main intellectual interests of his life and culminate (with* Bottle in the Sea) *in the religious speculations of a freethinker. A* Short History of the International Language Movement *was a pioneer treatise. It and* Europe Free and United—*together with work on the Committee to Frame a World Constitution—reflect a lifelong concern with European and world organization, and with problems of preserving the peace. This, as seen in daily conversation, in articles and in incessant letters of protest, was perhaps the central interest of his later life, though he was also constantly concerned about the suppression of minority opinions and rights, including those of American communists. But a book known only to a few American city planners, though much respected by French urbanistes, reflects Guérard's great avocation and labor of love. This was a humane yet highly technical study of city-planning problems,* L'Avenir de Paris, *published in Paris in 1959. In his last years Guérard returned to this treatise and wrote a wholly new and much expanded version.*

In the field of literature, Professor Guérard composed, in addition to the works cited above, Five Masters of French Romance, Honoré de Balzac *(in French),* Literature and Society, Art for Art's Sake, *and* Fossils and Presences. *Additional autobiographies include* Education of a Humanist *and* Testament of a Liberal. *His book of essays,* Beyond Hatred, *was written in 1925.*

I. Should the Historian Think About History?

> "I am too busy preaching the Gospel
> to worry about theology."
> — The Reverend Timothy Stone.

It may be a sin to be a millionaire: the excessive wealth of key words should be curbed, as well as the excessive wealth of key men. For riches beyond measure breed confusion, in the material, the intellectual and the moral worlds. It is confusion, not power, that corrupts; and absolute confusion corrupts absolutely.

A few familiar instances. The single term *love* covers a multitude of virtues and of sins. We need many words to discriminate between the mating instinct, brute lust, possessiveness, jealousy, sentimentality, affection, loyalty, and the supreme mystery, the supreme power, that St. Paul calls *charity*. We need an even richer gamut to cover wonder, awe, dread (the sacred sort), wishful thinking, rank superstition, crude magic, dead literalism, ecclesiasticism and ritual, metaphysics, esthetic enjoyment, the mores, the moral law within our hearts, and the mystic ecstasy—all of which, at various times, may claim the name of *religion*. If it be religion to roast a man alive, as Montaigne puts it, because he stumbles on the distinction between Homoousian and Homoiousian, or between consubstantiation and transsubstantiation, that religion is not the religion which, at various times, may claim the name of religion of Christ.

Democracy, in comparison, is a very simple concept: "We, the people . . . *Salus populi suprema lex esto* . . . *Vox populi* . . ." Yet in this country which believes itself to be democratic through and through, we find half a dozen strains of thought, diverse, inimical and inextricably entangled. First of all, there is the primitive, the prehuman herd instinct: the unreasoning stampede, the blind fury, the orgiastic explosions (the pogroms, the maffickings). We rationalize that instinct into hundred-percentism, loyalty to the American way of life, "My country right or wrong!"; and we organize an Inquisition to make sure that not a single lemming among us shall stray from the instinctive rush to the sea. Then there is the patriarchal-matriarchal reverence for age: treading in the footsteps of our ancestors, following the sacred tradition of the Founding Fathers, bowing to the wisdom of prejudice. The theocratic survives: we recognize that democratic slogans and machines are of no avail in those things that are not Caesar's. The technocratic asserts itself: when it comes to science, engineering, sanitation, medicine and—though not so consistently—to the interpretation of the law, "We, the people" bow to the opinion of experts: leave plumbing to plumbers and surgery to surgeons. Likewise the economic: political doctrines, even with the majesty of Eternal Verities, may blur but cannot destroy the essential fact: that Business is Business, and America's prime concern. Finally, we do not suppress, but rather we extol, the rugged individualism of Herbert Spencer and Herbert Hoover, the *libertarianism* which in truth, and literally, is anarchism. All radically different in principle, indeed antagonistic; all claiming to be facets of the great baroque jewel democracy.

Does *history* have a plain, single meaning, or is it, like love, religion, democracy, a writhing mass of irreconcilable concepts? This is a challenge, not a confession of despair. There is a way out, but it is arduous. The keys to the problem are relativity and pluralism. Truth may be found in rival hypotheses. The plain dealer may scorn subtle distinctions as casuistry. In the practical world, simplicity should prevail: transparent good will and clear-cut decisions. In the scientific, philosophical and spiritual domains, we should acknowledge the existence of infinite complexity. There are more than four "elements." There are more "faculties of the mind" than were dreamt of in old-fashioned psychology. There are more "senses" than the five which monopolize the name. There are more cardinal virtues and more deadly sins than the most learned Church Fathers could enumerate. Examined with scrupulous care, a plain motive may demand a formula more bewildering to the lay mind than any in organic chemistry. Our semantics reaches a degree of intricacy beyond the range of cybernetics. For even a million-dollar electronic brain will infallibly go wrong if it is asked absurd questions, if it is fed the wrong data, and if the results are read by the wrong mind.

Complexity, not confusion. Confusion may be in the nature of things, but I do not want to make it worse confounded. I do not gloat over chaos, the dwelling place of so many romantic minds: to me chaos is subhuman, while mystery is preterhuman. I do not accept an absurd universe: I crave order. I am a Cartesian: *Cogito ergo sum.* My sole warrant for believing in my own existence is my capacity to think. And to think is to project upon the world, boundless and inchoate, that *order* which is the very essence of my own mind. No retreat from the Enlightenment: rigorous honesty is still the best policy. No cult of the Dark Forces: our part is to curb or tame them. No escape into the Abyss, for that is sheer cowardice. Above all, no lazy meandering in the haze of make-believe. Analysis is a sustained fight against both the obvious and the indefinite. The achievement of Freud was not to recognize the existence of the Unconscious, which had been known through the ages; still less to proclaim the sovereignty of the Unconscious; but relentlessly to exorcise the Unconscious through the healing light of awareness.

So I cannot be satisfied with the holy simplicity of Ranke's dictum: *"Er will bloß zeigen wie es eigentlich gewesen."* (Needless to add that Ranke's practice far transcended his crude precept.) The catchword is the humble and innocent-looking *es:* we must first decide what is that protean *es* that Ranke modestly proposes to present. No doubt if you depart from the commonly accepted facts and concepts, the first result is a blur, and might even be a blank. This, however, should not discourage us. The example of the physical sciences ought to be reassuring. Compared with the rudimentary information and the simple laws I was taught in my youth, these sciences, for the lay mind, have grown intricate beyond comprehension and almost beyond belief. The uninitiated are bewildered; and the masters themselves, far from feeling more secure in their knowledge, are constantly discovering new depths in the unknown. I was on firmer ground at twelve than Einstein at the close of his career. Still, the amazing advance of the scientific mind breeds confidence, not despair. The cosmos grows mysterious beyond the boldest flights of metaphysicians and theologians; but over an ever-increasing area, we are imposing upon nature the reasoned pattern of our mind. We were able to say, Let the atom be shattered!—and lo! it was shattered. We may tomorrow reconstitute matter and energy according to the discipline of our intellect. We may, by taking thought, break the speed record of light. We may evolve new categories to supplant those weary conventions, time and space. We may fulfill Hegel's dream: the identity of the rational and the real. Provided we add: *Within the sphere of the human spirit;* and by this reservation, the outrageous paradox is turned into a truism. I can well imagine man shaping *his* universe in his own image. But what the universe is—or would be—without men to conceive it, I, being a man, have not the faintest conception. All knowledge grasped by man, evolved by man, is valid for man only, and is not binding on the angels.[1]

In more concrete terms, history is human; it selects and records those events which are shaped by men and shape the lives of men in return. Within that narrow compass—infinitesimal, I am ready to grant, but to us of infinite price—history is real and positive. The present reflections—my last Pisgah-sight of a domain which has fascinated me for three score years and ten—are not a universal *Que sçais-je?* I deny our capacity to grasp the absolute (else the absolute would be relative *to us*); but within the bournes of our conscious life, there are definite ways for us to learn some of the things we want to know, and to make use of such knowledge. I am an activist and a pragmatist, not a cloud-weaver. Deliberately, I have attempted to turn thoughts that were vaguely clear—nationalism, genius, inspiration, Providence—into thoughts that were clearly vague. But skepticism was the tool, not the goal. To dispel phantoms is a step in purposive action.

My faith in history is firm. It is firm because it is simple, and, I may proudly add, naïve: The aim of history is to seek justice, and, as the sole path to justice, to ascertain truth. Righteousness, blinded by its own glow, is apt to ignore the pertinent facts. On the other hand, there is noth-

---

[1] The idea that the ultimate particles of the universe may be units of thought, and not units of matter, is well expressed in Werner Heisenberg's "Die philosophische Probleme der Atomphysik" (*L'Homme et l'Atome,* Neuchatel, 1958), 37–53. And Heisenberg shows that the problem had already been stated by the Greeks. Mathematics offers a picture, not of the universe without, but of the human mind.

ing so stupid as a fact, unless it finds its proper place in a just order.[2] I am chary of Schiller's famous phrase, *"Die Weltgeschicte ist das Weltgericht,"* because it has echoes of a theodicy which I do not find convincing. Pare it to the bone, cut out the *Welt* we cannot grasp, and it makes incontrovertible sense: History is judgment. Schiller's dictum, however, fails to tell us according to what law such a judgment is rendered. We can easily imagine Kafka's *Trial* as a despairing vision of history: the charge, the law, the court, the judge, all veiled in tragic darkness. But legions of facts picked at random will not save us. Beyond the murk in which Kafka himself was lost, I see a gleam. *Solvitur ambulando:* the striving for the law—the will to justice—is itself the only law.

II. All the World's a Stage

History is at one and the same time the whole course of human events—the very few among those events which are conspicuous for their significance[3]—and the piecing together of those few events so as to form a consistent, an intelligible sequence. To *be* history, to *make* history, to *write* history are three different things; and on all three planes there are elusive variations.

In the most general sense, then, history is the sum total of all the facts which affect human life. If this be accepted, astronomy, geology, biology, and even secondary sciences

---

[2] We might apply to historical criticism the well-worn legal formula which I learned from Perry Mason: Objected to as irrelevant, incompetent and immaterial. Objection sustained.

[3] "It is only the decision of the historian to use them, the conviction of the historian that they are significant for his purpose, which makes them into the 'facts of history'." E. H. Carr, *The New Society* (London, 1951), 9.

like climatology and bacteriology, must be regarded as historical. In Genesis, the creation of the heavens and of the earth is reported in the same matter-of-fact tone as the birth of Seth and of Enos: in Ranke's words, this is "how it actually happened." Voltaire and H. G. Wells, in a slightly different spirit, followed the same magnificent pattern. The murk of protohistory deepens into the palpable darkness of prehistory; prehistory in its turn leads us to prehuman evolution; which posits (and does not explain) the origin of life; which ultimately raises the nebular hypothesis. No wonder most historians prefer starting *in medias res*. But thus to ignore the past is to produce journalism, not history. The remotest prehistory is still with us. The brutal instincts which might well be the original sin of mankind now assume the elaborate techniques of diplomacy and warfare; but they were ancient in the paleolithic age. Who knows? We may be still paying the price for taking the wrong turn untold eons ago: at least this is the theory advanced by Rousseau in his *Discourse on the Origin of Inequality*. But Rousseau, with his grand gesture—"First of all, let us brush aside 'the facts!'"—is not in good repute among professional historians.

Facts affecting human life! Within a narrower framework than astronomy, geology or biology, it can hardly be denied that a slow change in humidity or temperature counts for infinitely more than the most elaborate maneuvers of Talleyrand or Bismarck, than the lightning campaigns of Napoleon or Hitler. The despised microbe is a scourge of God more deadly than Attila. History written by medical men would be more realistic than history written by politicians. Hans Zinsser was justified in offering us *Rats, Lice and History*, for rats and lice affect human destiny more potently than Laval or Quisling ever did. W. H. S. Jones ascribed to malaria the decline of stamina in the Hellenistic world. It was measles, not warfare, that turned the vigorous Hawaiians into an ethnic minority in their own lovely islands. Standard history does not wholly ignore such factors. But even the Black Death gets scant notice compared with kings' mistresses. The chroniclers of our own age pass lightly over the fact that, at the time of the First World War, the flu took a heavier toll than the battlefields.

If the microbe is a historic character of commanding magnitude, what shall we say of the gene? Much as I oppose the crude application of the race idea in political history, as expounded by Gobineau, Vacher de Lapouge, Houston Stuart Chamberlain, Madison Grant, and even by sounder thinkers such as Otto Seek or David Starr Jordan, there is in it a substratum, at the same time stubborn and elusive, which we cannot *a priori* refuse to investigate. Nils Larsen is attempting to trace migrations through the distribution of blood types. Mendel, Morgan, Beedle might be safer guides in political history than Machiavelli.

As for changes in technique, and the resulting changes in social structure, their impact on human life is obvious. Who will appraise the great paleolithic revolution? The dawn of agriculture and cattle breeding, the first start of metallurgy? And in the last three centuries, the machine age, the new scientific era? The rough engines of Newcomen and Cowley were of immensely greater moment than the insane pride of Louis XIV, the backstairs intrigues at Queen Anne's court, the dazzling victories of Marlborough. James Watt altered the conditions of human life, as Napoleon did not.

For centuries, the importance of vast, anonymous, perhaps even nonhuman processes has been acknowledged by students of human affairs. Jean Bodin and Montesquieu evolved the theory of climates. Michelet gave a geographical survey of France, the body of that entity which to him was a person. Renan, in his Syrian mission, studied what he called the Fifth Gospel: the physical environment which according to him gave color and substance to the figure of Christ. He carried the "climatic" theory so far as to declare (against a formidable host of facts) that "the desert is monotheistic."

Historians therefore cannot be accused of ignoring those factors which are not consciously man-made. Yet they accept the nonpersonal view with barely concealed resistance. In their eyes, such an approach is characteristic of sociology and anthropology, not of history proper. All nonhuman, impersonal, unconscious elements are merely the background of history. That background might well be taken for granted, or, if presented at all, it should remain subdued. What matters to the historian is the strutting of actual personages, with distinctive features and costumes, and lights trained upon them to bring their figures into sharper relief. For Dryasdust in his heart is closer to Shakespeare than to Lyell, Pasteur or Mendel. To him, "all the world's a stage," and history a drama.

Like tragedy, history deals with human destiny in human terms, that is to say in terms of will and passion. Its very essence is consciousness: a fact becomes historical only when men are definitely aware of its existence and of its significance. Note that this awareness need not be contemporaneous with the event: it may be retrospective or prospective. We shall see that hope and dread, the phantoms of things past, the shape of things to come, are historical factors: it is they that *make* history. So history as it exists in the human mind does not follow a smooth and even a chronological course. Our perspective is constantly changing. When we tell "how it actually happened," we re-create our past, we anticipate our future. Pontius Pilate, in Anatole France's tale *The Procurator of Judea,* had forgotten Jesus: but the world today remembers. So we have rediscovered, without giving it a name, the greater Renaissance of the eleventh century; and we are inclined to consider the reformations of the Cluniacs and of the Franciscans more "epoch-making" than those of Luther and Calvin. As figures from the past come into focus and impose themselves upon our consciousness, so other figures grow faint and may dissolve altogether. How many rulers, ministers, commanders, once mighty in their own conceit, have faded away like Ozymandias, king of kings?

History is collective memory. What is it that makes men and events historical, that is to say *memorable?* Frankly, their dramatic, their sensational character. I know that a mere shock of surprise, a vogue or a panic, may fail to achieve a permanent place in history. The Great Fear, in the stormy dawn of the French Revolution, has left but faint traces, vivid as it was at the time. An event must have magnitude and duration: deep and prolonged echoes. But, as the collective mind is sluggish, the shock is all but indispensable: it provides the *quantum,* to borrow, and probably distort, Planck's term. No shock, no history: serenely happy people have none; neither have unhappy people, if their misery is habitual and dull. The commonplace, which makes up the bulk of our existence, has no standing in history. Sociology must be statistical: history deals with the unique, not with the average. A profound change, unnoticed, is not historical: there may be chemical alterations taking place in the atmosphere or in our blood cells that will radically alter our conditions of life: who knows, and therefore who cares? An episode, if it impresses itself upon our imagination, attains the dignity—perhaps I should say the fascination—of history. But note this contrast: Statistics tell us that automobile accidents are responsible for more deaths, within the same span of time and in proportion to the population, than the French Terror at its height. These deaths are tragic enough; they engage the responsibility of men, individually and as a community. But in a statistical report, the individual dramas are obliterated. There is no terror or pity in columns of figures. The Terror was deliberate; it was intended to impress, and it did impress. Had there been only a handful of victims— the king, the queen, the Girondists, Danton—it would still remain a lurid page; and it ended with a crash of poetic justice: the downfall of the fanatical tyrant. Death by collision is more cruel than the humane contraption of Dr. Guillotin. But our imagination is not focused, and therefore it is not fired. Statistics cannot be fused into an epic drama.

From these familiar premises, we may draw a few fairly obvious conclusions. In the first place, the only historical law is that history has no law. William Bennet Munro liked to say, "We can teach history, but history cannot teach us." H. A. L. Fisher, a particularly level-headed Briton, in his vast survey of the European field, could find no trace of purpose, design, inevitable causality. Karl R. Popper denounced the poverty of historicism—by which he meant the delusion that history could ever predict with the certainty of science. All the philosophies of history, including the impressive modern attempts of Oswald Spengler (*The Decline of the West*), of Nicholas Berdyaev (*The Meaning of History*), of Ortega y Gasset (*Toward a Philosophy of History*) and, mightiest of all, of Arnold Toynbee (*A Study of History*), are but elaborate self-portraits, using as their medium a cunning mosaic of historical facts.

In the second place, there is no relation whatever between intellectual and moral values, on the one hand, and, on the other, a place in history. A good man in private life does not reach the threshold of historical consciousness: a scoundrel may achieve sinister eminence. Even in high places, the world remembers a Nero or a Caligula far more vividly than an Antoninus Pius. The test is effective drama, not sense or sensibility; the key word is glamor, not virtue or service.

Egomaniacs of all kinds, profiteers as well as prophets, have a peculiar tendency: they crave the limelight, and therefore they occupy it. The troupe of the great historical show has a number of stock characters. The conqueror, of course, even Tamburlaine the Great; the woman of irresistible and fatal beauty—Helen of Troy, Cleopatra, Mary Queen of Scots, and in the "age of reason," Madame de Pompadour, Madame du Barry, Marie-Antoinette (Burke fell into that trap); the villain—Nero, Richard III, Marat, Fouché, Goebbels and maybe Stalin; the refulgent spendthrift, "the host with the most"—Francis I at Fontainebleau or Chambord, Louis XIV at Versailles; the rake—Don Juan, Marshal de Richelieu, or that Casanova with a crown, Louis XV and his Parc-aux-Cerfs.

On the whole, history is not overfond of the happy ending. It revels in tragedy. Perhaps the true name for this sadistic craving is *Schadenfreude* or subconscious malice. Perhaps, if we take a less cynical view of human nature, the death of the wicked is poetic justice, and the death of the innocent in martyrdom, the test of unselfish devotion. Martyrdom, however, is no argument: men have suffered torture and death for the worst causes as well as for the best. Mussolini and Hitler were martyrs. Once in a while a weakling, a common man, may qualify, if there is a pathetic contrast between his position and his capacity: Louis XVI for one. All too rarely, pure figures survive with a halo: St. Louis, Joan of Arc, Lincoln: but martyrdom, which is melodrama, was necessary to their prestige.

A success story may close in quiet dignity: Frederick II, with no abatement to his glory, ended his days in the Philistine character of a good administrator; and there was no meretricious aura about George Washington. Still, they had gone through tragedy at Kunersdorf and Valley Forge. The tremor of terror and pity had been felt. On the strength of that, they were allowed to live happily ever after. Tragedy, not triumph, is the key to Napoleon's inexhaustible appeal. His most prestigious campaigns were utter failures: in Egypt, in Russia, he abandoned his army to its fate. Had he been permitted to end his days as a gentleman farmer in Shropshire, the hero-worship which still inspires hundreds of books every year would have been greatly diminished. He needed a Caucasus; he cast himself in the part of Prometheus, and poor Sir Hudson Lowe in the role of the vulture.

For the protagonists, as a rule, are at least obscurely conscious that history is drama: they dramatize themselves; they play their part. Napoleon was, of course, the perfect play-actor, ready to perform any role, provided it brought him applause. History, however, despises the mere *histrion* all costume, posture and claptrap. Few people even in Germany took William II seriously as the Vicar of God on earth, the heir of Barbarossa, the overlord of Europe, the defender of Western culture against the Yellow Peril, the Wagnerian hero in whom both Christ and Wotan were well pleased. The trappings were too obviously borrowed, the mountings were trite: yet but for the miracle of the Marne, he might have stolen the show. Hitler appealed to the same spirit, but at a deeper level; and he did become a force, not merely a carnival figure.

In some cases the theatrical aspect, although undeniable,

is so superficial that it merely elicits a smile and does not seriously affect our esteem. I am confident that Kitchener, Pershing and MacArthur were able commanders, although they played to perfection the military hero, every inch a soldier, as Joffre, Galliéni, Foch, Marshall, Eisenhower did not. Louis XIV was not merely, as in Thackeray's cartoon, a pitiful Ludovicus encased in a buckram Rex: he was a single entity, Ludovicus Rex, through and through and at every moment. In secular history as well as in religion, it is hard at times to draw the line between the service of a cause and its ritual. At military parade, the blare of brass bands, the return of the conquering heroes, the altar to the Unknown Soldier, the shrines of great men, the monuments to great events, a solemn burial, a coronation: all this is confessedly, even blatantly stagey, yet it is effective and probably inevitable. The dramatic ceases to be purely histrionic when it is sincere, when the man plays his own part with conviction, be it that of prophet, founder of a religion, Führer, Duce, Peerless Leader; when the role he assumes is in accord with his own ideal; when faith, *persona* and personality are fused into one. Perhaps Mahatma Gandhi is the clearest example (outside of Christian history) of such a miraculous harmony.

The borderland cases are interesting to study. Franklin noticed in Paris that he was expected to be, not the diplomat of the familiar kind, but at one and the same time the virtuous Quaker, the Child of Nature, the Noble Savage, and the hero of science: everything, in fact, that the gilded Court parasites were not. He tried on a Court dress, found it awkward, and shrewdly decided to give the Parisian public what they wanted. He dressed and talked the complex part to perfection. For effect no doubt, and to his own glory; but above all, because it best served the interests of his country, and because, with all its paradoxical contradictions, it was actually true. *To play a part is to be conscious of a secret or obvious consistency.* So Henry IV and Abraham Lincoln, like Franklin, contributed without effort to their own legends. They did not "put it on," but they were careful not to step out of character. Theodore Roosevelt composed for himself a bluff, strenuous, hearty personage, not in harmony with his ancestry, his education or even his physique; he kept it up for twenty years with hardly a false note. Franklin Roosevelt managed to combine, with a skill far beyond the crude cleverness of Hollywood, a richly shaded, elusive yet consistent personage. He was the friend of the people (like Marat) with a Groton accent, the starry-eyed reformer who could shrewdly manipulate a party machine; it was said that he had a rendezvous with destiny, but stopped on the way to square it with Jim Farley. Not a few tried to hiss him off the stage; but the public wanted three or four repeat performances. Against him Herbert Hoover, who had nothing to offer but rigidity of thought, stiffness of manners and a cult of efficiency, had no shadow of a chance. It took twenty-five years of retirement to make America realize that Mr. Hoover was actually human.[4]

Lord Curzon, according to Harold Nicolson, liked to give his "justly famous impersonation of So-and-So impersonating Lord Curzon"; and undoubtedly, for sixty years, Winston Churchill has given the grateful world a masterly rendering of that perennial stage favorite, Winston Church-

---

[4] The reticence that hampered Mr. Hoover can be turned into an asset. Napoleon, one of the most voluble rulers in history, created the legend of the strong, silent man: "I command, or keep silent." Coolidge, Cool Cal the Tactiturn, made his verbal parsimony part of the American folklore: he might have been even more of a popular figure if like Harpo Marx he had been totally dumb.

ill: Marlborough, Chatham and John Bull combined, with dashes of Bernard Shaw, overtones of Angela Thirkell, and stray hints from dear old *Punch:* the richest, mellowest and most potent composition in the history of the drama.

Conversely, some very clever, very good and at times very great characters failed to dramatize themselves, to capture the limelight. Everybody, in France at any rate, knows that the military miracle of the French Revolution was the work of Lazare Carnot, the Organizer of Victory. Carnot evolved a new strategy, taking full advantage of the two great assets of the young Republic—massive manpower and enthusiasm. He conceived vast plans, implemented by competent staff work, which in three years snatched victory out of disaster. Napoleon inherited the prestige, the self-confidence, the organization, the personnel of Carnot's armies; and in twenty years, he lost everything that France had won by 1795. Yet even in France, Lazare Carnot is but a name. His remains lie in the Pantheon, but attract no pilgrims. Some remember him solely as the grandfather of President Sadi Carnot. He secured no rank and no wealth for himself, and no halo either.

Louis-Philippe attempted with extraordinary pertinacity a most difficult part: the reconciler, the blender of traditions, the crowned head who is also the best of republicans, the royal prince deftly shifting from sword and scepter to that symbol of prudence and ecenomy, the umbrella; the drab, stay-at-home bourgeois who gave France the romantic spectacle of colorful warfare in Algeria; the believer in peace-at-any-price who sought to capture the effulgence of Napoleon's glory by cultivating the legend for all it was worth—and a great deal more. The part was intricate beyond Louis-Philippe's famed sagacity. Perhaps the great actor lacked the proper degree of naïveté: for to be fully convincing an artist must, at climactic moments, be taken in by his own performance. The public remained inert. The final verdict was spoken by Lamartine: "France is bored." Louis-Philippe was yawned off the stage.

I count among the stage failures the Hero of Two Worlds, Lafayette. He won fame when he was barely adolescent. He was right then: his correspondence with Washington, highly creditable to both, could still be the *vade mecum* of liberal statesmanship. He remained faithful to his early ideal; and sensible historians—if there were any—must be expected to conclude, "Ah! if only the rulers of opinion in 1789, in 1792, in 1815, had rallied to the sane, moderate, generous programme of Lafayette!" But somehow he failed to intrigue the public mind. His popularity, which was immense at times, never hardened into authority. His chivalrous disinterestedness was partly to blame: he never attempted to seize personal power. Partly he lost out because he was too obviously right: and we fail to make the vital distinction between the obvious and the commonplace. He was too far ahead of cynics like Talleyrand, Fouché, Barras; of fanatics of the right and of the left, like Marie-Antoinette, Marat, Robespierre; of men whose lives and thoughts were a turbid stream, but who for that very reason, were vivid and dramatic: Mirabeau, Danton. Not priggish, still he appears as the Sir Charles Grandison of his age. And to the present day, the mode among historians is to dismiss him with a condescending smile. One act of unscrupulous violence, inevitably leading to disaster, and he might have achieved a place among the glamorous characters of history.

III. Identity of History and Legend

I have insisted so far on the individual character in the drama of history: hero or villain, vampire or martyr. This does not mean that I believe with Carlyle in the decisive importance of "heroes," luminous or somber, of "providential men," [5] of Scourges of God. Not merely because I am convinced that sociological change is far deeper than the thrilling drama on the well-lit and carefully set stage; but because, in a drama, situation counts for more than character. In a masterpiece, they blend. But a play with a breathless plot will entrance an audience—not excluding professional scholars—even though the *dramatis personae* are as rudimentary, as conventional as those of Alexander Dumas and the Commedia dell'Arte. Whereas without startling events, discoveries, reversals, false hopes, miraculous strokes of fate, catastrophe or apotheosis, a problem on the purely psychological plane has no chance of popular success. If *Hamlet* entrances us as a probing of human destiny, that is because it has survived, like *Oedipus,* as a supreme whodunit, a thumping melodrama. Even at the extreme limit, Molière's *Misanthrope,* never such a favorite with the general public as his stagey *Tartuffe,* presents a man in a particular and absurd *situation,* and vainly attempting to find his way out. If the apostle of blunt sincerity had not fallen in love with a young coquette, there would have been no play whatever. There may be more psychology in Amiel's *Journal* than in *Oedipus, Hamlet, The Misanthrope* or *Faust*: but there is no *story.*

So it is with that story on the grand scale that we call history. Who cares for a great character—I have known not a few—who never had to face a crisis? The crisis, on the contrary, appeals to us on its own merits, even if the characters are frankly commonplace. In the highest art, I repeat, personage and situation react on each other:

---

[5] Napoleon III's expression and thesis in the famous preface to his *Life of Caesar.*

events will reveal or mature a character; the character is a factor in the chain of events. History is less exacting: the Spirit Ironic who stages our annals is not a playwright of the highest order.

At times, history will force the part of a hero on a modest individual who had not craved the embarrassing honor. With every loyal American, "I like Ike"; but, be it said to his credit, he is the reverse of a Napoleon, a Hitler, a Stalin. At least until the eve of his accession to power, he was conscious of his limitations. But *ex officio* the Commander in Chief of the greatest array of forces in history, and the most sweepingly victorious, must be of heroic mold: the situation creates the part. And Eisenhower, uneasily at first, and with an apologetic smile, had to get used to his refulgent halo. Who knows? He may have become convinced that such a destiny must be the result of some inner power. Gastounet Doumergue, the perfect model of the average politician, was picked out in a crisis to be the Strong Man of France—an outrageous instance of miscasting. But in a few weeks he almost persuaded himself that he was that man, and a frown of determination, almost worthy of Mussolini, effaced his humorous Southern smile. When the situation requires a hero, a hero must be provided. Uruguay, a particularly sane community, discovered that a Founding Father, a Washington, a Bolívar, an Ataturk, was indispensable to a self-respecting nation; so, scanning its meager annals, it picked out Artigas, who will do as well as any. When not even a Doumergue or an Artigas is at hand, a hero is manufactured out of whole cloth. The slow and obscure epic of Swiss independence demanded a central character: so out of a vague Northern legend, two hundred years after the event, William Tell came into being, complete with apple-shooting and steering a boat in the storm. Not a few biographies of William Tell were unaware of their apocryphal character: they "told how it actually happened." Perhaps such apocrypha are more profoundly historical, in molding the faith of a people, than the record of the confused events which, by imperceptible steps, made Switzerland a reality. In *making* history, no fact-finder will ever rival Schiller's drama.

So, as a rule, a situation will force a protagonist into the limelight. Not necessarily an individual: the hero may by anonymous or even collective. In 1794 a French vessel, *Le Vengeur,* was isolated and exposed to the fire of the whole British squadron. The crew chose death rather than surrender, fired a last volley while the decks were already awash, nailed the tricolor to the shattered mast, and went down singing the *Marseillaise.* The sublime story was told by Carlyle with the vividness of a gifted eye-witness; in the form of a marble monument, it is perpetuated in the Paris Pantheon; it is confirmed in that treasure house of the half-educated, *Le Petit Larousse.* The name of the heroic captain is forgotten, while we remember Casabianca ("The boy stood on the burning deck . . ."). It is just as well: for Carlyle discovered afterwards that the whole episode had been manufactured by Barrère. The *Vengeur* had surrendered two hours before sinking; and when it finally disappeared, the French captain was eating mutton pie at his vanquisher's table.

History, as presented by historians, is a well-made play: not a pageantry of detached episodes, but a situation, with exposition, growth, crisis. Aristotle himself preferred melodrama to tragedy in its frigid purity: he wanted in a play those sudden changes of fortune which inspire us with terror and pity. The tragedy proceeds to its inexorable end:

but suspense, or dramatic interest, requires that at every step we might believe that the choice is still open, that it might yet be otherwise. And the end must bring catharsis: the grand final chord, glorious or somber, which gives the key to the whole drama, and turns it into an organic whole.

Once again, no better play (on the popular level) was ever conceived than the career of Napoleon. The coronation and Austerlitz are brilliant moments; but they do not affect us so deeply as the retreat from Moscow, the superb desperate campaign of 1814, the incredible gamble of the Hundred Days, the long captivity in St. Helena. What moves us is not sheer luck, and still less the just reward of sane and steady endeavor: it is the titanic wrestling with fate. And what unique variety in the scenes, what abundance of supers, what opulence in the stage properties! Egypt, the Tuileries, Notre Dame, Moscow in flames, snow falling implacably as though it were an instrument of the gods, the remote and lonely rock, the Arch of Triumph, the splendid pageant of the Second Burial, the sarcophagus of porphyry under the gilded dome! The hero himself, while not despicable, was not of the highest quality; but he knew how, in every word and gesture, to extract the utmost stage effect out of a given situation. Like the masters of mass communication in our time, he appeals shamelessly to the greatest number. Philosophers and prophets have been urging us for two thousand years to rise above the subhuman instinct to fight: but we are reluctant to give up the marvelous drama.

Detached events, as noted in chronicles, annals, diaries and newspapers, provide only the raw material of history. Three conditions are essential to transmute Mrs. Grundy into Clio. First of all, there must be a modicum of belief that the thing actually happened: Ranke's famous dictum remains a sure foundation. The public mind, however, is not too exacting on this point: it is satisfied with the willing suspension of disbelief. Legends hover happily between fact and fiction. Adults cherish figures as syncretic and improbable as Santa Claus. No enquirer deserves the name of historian unless he is equipped with the critical spirit, which dissolves romance. But historians with a religious, racial or national bias apply the critical acid with such care and skill that it will not be a menace to vital illusions. Professors in the most orthodox seminaries know far more about the textual and chronological problems of the Bible than Voltaire ever did. Masson, Kircheisen, Madelin are aware of every flaw in Napoleon's character, of every blunder in his career, far more than Barni, Duret or "Jean Savant." We still speak of our secession from England as "great and glorious" and of the struggle for Southern independence as a crime. Most "scientific" histories are legends robed in true facts.

The second condition is a certain degree of magnitude, in time and space. The parochial and the ephemeral, *per se,* leave no impression. The village Hampden shares the fate of the mute inglorious Milton: he remains in limbo. There are cases in which *magnitude* is not *grandeur,* but sheer mass: any child can build a pyramid, but the Pharaohs created a record. The colossal may be vulgar, but it is an argument. No expedition could have been worse conceived, worse prepared or worse executed than Napoleon's Russian campaign. It took no genius to lose six hundred thousand men in a Russian winter: we have at least a dozen generals who could have rivaled such an achievement. But there is an epic quality about sheer numbers. A blunder is foolishness if it causes the loss of a patrol: it becomes a *Götterdämmerung* if it engulfs an army.

The third condition is the most essential and the most elusive: *response*. Events count, not because of their authenticity or magnitude, but because of the emotion they rouse. A single miscarriage of justice, in the case of Captain Dreyfus, created a storm which shook French society and echoed throughout the world. That emotion depends on imponderable factors. The same explosive mixture may ignite in one case and fizzle in another. The sinking of the *Maine* was merely an incident: but the martial spirit was ready to flare up. On the other hand, England chose not to go to war with Russia over the far more perilous Doggerbank affair. John Bull is as proud and as pugnacious as Uncle Sam. But in 1898 America was a lusty young giant, eager to step on the world stage; whereas in 1904 England was still feeling the weariness of the Boer War. Besides, Russia was the ally of France, with whom England was seeking to establish a chlorotic *entente cordiale*.

The task of the historian, as I see it, is to analyze such a response. Most writers assume tacitly that it is spontaneous and unanimous. The readiness to fight and perish demonstrates the existence of a collective entity—tribe or nation, racial, religious or social group—greater than any of its members. Treitschke spoke of the "holy wrath" that swept over Germany in 1893 with the Liberation crusade, forgetting that many Germans—even many Prussians—had fought bravely under Napoleon's standards. Hitler embodied the burning resentment created by the *Diktat* (even though the Locarno agreements had superseded it) and by the Polish Corridor festering in the sacred flesh of the Fatherland. At what moment does that response become a definite fact? At one moment, to borrow Walter Lippmann's terms, does the Phantom Public achieve the authority of the Public Mind?

Vox populi is never articulate: it cannot even repeat, but only endorse with a confused clamor the words uttered by the few. There must be leaders, even though they be obscure and nameless. Someone—and it need not have been Camille Desmoulins—was the first to say in the Palais Royal, "To the Bastille!" But that intermediate step—the initiative assumed by a few—although essential, is not decisive. It merely pushes the problem one step farther back: it is not the immediate response to the events, but rather the response to the interpreters of the events. And that response is by no means inevitable. In 1898—and in 1776—the martial spirit burst into flames; and it might have been otherwise. But William Randolph Hearst, who was supposed to wield immense power, urged for many years that we should teach Mexico a lesson; and the only results were two futile gestures. Ever since 1917, many Americans have earnestly preached the Hitler gospel: Soviet Russia must be destroyed. In both cases, the public mind could not be pressured to the point of ignition and explosion.

When the People's Voice is heard at last, it does not prove that the people is right. It does not even prove that there is such an entity as the people. "America sternly resolved . . ." is a figment. Tribes, churches, nations have always been compelled to enforce taboos and beliefs, to suppress dissent, doubts and even misgivings, as disloyalty, heresy, treason. Clemenceau's policy was pithily summed up: "All good Frenchmen are with me for war to the bitter end; all bad Frenchmen will be shot." We need no such extreme measure: but every American who thinks for himself is branded as un-American.

Why do minorities—and at times majorities—allow themselves to be silenced? Terror is not the only answer.

No government could cow free men into submission. Even if Caudillo Franco had more inquisitors and more executioners at his service, he could not have suppressed the proud and vigorous Spanish people for two decades. The key to that enigma is, I repeat, to be found in dramatic appeal. A group has a good chance of remaining in control so long as it speaks in no uncertain voice, so long as it offers a picture that is definite and colorful. The opposition is doomed to futility if it presents only a blurred image, an uncertain path, an invertebrate policy. The opponents of Mussolini, Hitler, Franco, Stalin, discouraged by their previous failures and their irremediable divisions, had no clear-cut alternative to propose. They were powerless because they were, literally, *insignificant,* meaningless. The "liberals" in America are a welter of ambiguities. The leaders of the Fourth French Republic were on the whole well-meaning, honest and able: but they could only fumble and stumble. De Gaulle, on the other hand, had a well-made drama in readiness: a character, a situation, a purpose. In literature and in politics, the amorphous is always wrong.

The key word in history is therefore *significance,* or symbolical value. The symbol is never of a clear-cut thought, a well-defined interest: these can be expressed literally; they need not and cannot be dramatized. The symbol stands for "phantasmal hopes and fears." Intrinsically, it may be of little worth: what is a flag but a piece of bunting tacked to a pole? Why should we go to the very brink of war for Quemoy or Matsu? If *Homo economicus* or *Homo sapiens* (there is a distinction, and a difference) did rule the world, history as we make it, enjoy it and write it would cease; it would yield the study of human affairs to sociology.

Heroes and their deeds are part of folklore: they are

memorable because they are vivid, because they *mean* more than they *are,* and *evoke* more than they mean. Vico was right: legends, despised by the rationalist, are the keys of human action in the past. They contain a more essential truth than an array of plain meaningless facts: if by truth we understand virtue, potency. For the religious-minded as well as for the arrant pragmatist, that which fails to work is not true. Scholarly research never makes a dent on a living faith, because faith is a promise of power. That which is technically accurate but impotent is irrelevant, and if introduced into history, actually delusive.

But the principle of Vico applies not merely to the dim reaches of protohistory, the age of gods and heroes; it was at work throughout the fitful light of conscious history; and it is alive today. Historical persons, historical institutions and events are those which have assumed the prestige and the potency of a legend. Note that a legend implies an aura of fascination, but does not posit approval. There is an enthusiasm of assent, and an enthusiasm of horror. Perhaps evil is, paradoxically, more positive than good, as dread may be more vivid than hope. Most religions are a system of exorcism against the devil. The average American who so unresistingly followed his leader to the brink of war had no positive faith in John Foster Dulles: he believed, shudderingly and primarily, in Lenin-Stalin-Khrushchev as an infernal trinity, and only secondarily in Dulles as the archangel who could save us from their clutches.

Response, significance, potency, symbol: men, institutions, causes impress themselves as historical realities only when they stand for some dream or passion greater than mere physical existence. A hero is more than flesh and blood; a faith is more than an ecclesiastical establishment;

a cause is more than a party machine; a culture is more than a catalogue of taboos; a nation is more than territory and government. In the Platonic sense, they are *ideas*, of which material events are but the blurred and distorted shadows. Or they are *myths*, which alone impart meaning to phenomena. And it is for myths, not for bread, that men fight and die.

This is clearest in the case of nations, the essential characters in the historical drama. Nations are not actual facts: they are articles of faith. Nature did not create and does not maintain the United States: the United States *is* because of our belief. If that faith should grow faint, the United States would lose virtue, or power; if it were to fade away altogether, the United States would disappear from history. Two contrasted cases will elucidate this apparent paradox. The Congo Free State had all the appurtenances and paraphernalia of a country: territory, flag, sovereign, laws, a police force, civil servants. Yet the world felt that all this, rigged up in the name of philanthropy, was but a mask for exploitation. No one, least of all the shrewd profiteer Leopold II, ever believed in the Congo Free State. When it vanished, there was a sigh of relief.

On the other hand, Poland, torn asunder by the three imperial vultures, ceased to exist on the map and in the eyes of the law. It survived as a spirit: in the tragic memories and millennial hopes of the Poles themselves; in the shame and resentment of Europe ("so long as Poland is enslaved, Europe shall live in a state of mortal sin"); in the uneasy conscience of her tormentors: her ghost was ever present at their feast. Repeatedly, that indomitable ghost attempted to force its way back onto the stage: in the Grand Duchy of Warsaw, in the autonomous kingdom under Alexander I, in abortive insurrections, in the ramshackle empire of Pilsudski. Its ill-compacted body has expanded and shrunk. But there always was a Poland; and there is a Poland today.

So the substance of history is not to be found in the *Statesman's Yearbook,* but in the imagination and in the heart of men. History is legend, symbol and myth. Its rules are those not of political economy, but of epic drama (which is an acceptable definition of Greek tragedy). Between history and fiction, *Wahrheit und Dichtung,* there is a profound identity which sets them apart from statistical science, social or physical, and from the pure logic of mathematics.

Closely akin yet—I admit—different; but the boundaries between them are hard to trace. On the more obvious plane, there are the enormous fields of historical romance and romanced history, far more popular than history proper. But even for the scholar who severely rejects fiction, are there no twilight zones? What gods in the annals of mankind had objective existence? Did King Arthur actually rule? Is the Charlemagne we remember that of the epic, in the eleventh century, or that of the chronicles, in the ninth, or a strange hybrid? Is Artigas more alive than William Tell? Which Napoleon, still inspiring research works and romances by the hundred, is the more real: the technician, the efficiency expert, or the Promethean myth that the romanticists placed in their teeming pantheon, by the side of Faust, Don Juan and the Wandering Jew? [6]

Shall we say that in pure history (as in orthodox religion), full belief is expected, while in poetry make-believe suffices? And that history—as we shall see—is a motive

---

[6] It is notable that Grabbe wrote, in the same spirit, a drama on *Don Juan und Faust,* and one on *Napoleon oder die Hundert Tage;* and Edgar Quinet an *Ahasverus,* a *Napoléon* and a *Prométhée.*

(rather than a guide) for action, while poetry exists for our enjoyment? No doubt the Schiller of *Die Räuber* did not follow quite the same rules as the Schiller of *Geschichte des Dreissigjärigen Kriegs*, with *Wallenstein, Die Jungfrau von Orleans* and *Wilhelm Tell* hovering in the middle mist. But the distinction wavers. Don Quixote believed in the romances of chivalry more firmly than we now believe in the earlier books of Livy; and he was guided by them. Sane and learned men accept the literal authenticity of the Book of Jonah. The *Marseillaise* was worth an army to the Revolution. *Uncle Tom's Cabin* was a decisive victory that prepared the way for Gettysburg.

So, by a circuitous route, we return to our revered master Ranke. The historian should attempt to tell us, without fabrication or prevarication, how it actually happened. But he must never forget that *it* is made up of passions and dreams, of myths and legends, which alone give human events their significance. In the beginning was not the word, not the deed, but the pain, the love and the dread.

IV. Vital Myths Are Prospective

Let the dead bury their dead.

There is a tradition in the House of Commons that no member is ever to be mentioned by name. Charles Fox asked the Speaker, "What would happen if I did?" The Speaker answered, in tones of religious awe, "God only knows." And the great radical bowed meekly to the wisdom of prejudice.

The historical spirit is often confounded with tradition. The hallowed past has a power far beyond the charm of quaintness. It appears not to the antiquarian merely, but to the philosopher. Rootless men, institutions and nations may live for the day: the deeper realities exist *in time*. They achieve an organic harmony through imperceptible growth. The duty of man, as an individual, and above all as a political or religious leader, is to resist conscious and willful change. Planning is worse than foolishness: it is blasphemy. The will of God is manifested only through *vis inertiae*.

This very ancient doctrine—the Middle Ages in particular were committed to the sacredness of *custom*—was reasserted by Burke as a reaction against the Enlightenment. Voltaire had told Rousseau, "No one could spend more wit in attempting to turn us into dumb animals," and Carlyle was to pour forth Niagaras of turgid eloquence in praise of silence. In the same fashion, Burke lavished treasures of lucid, cogent thought on the apology of unthinking. His were the reflections to end all reflections. The man who takes thought, like the woman who deliberates, is lost.

This obscurantist[7] doctrine has been revived, intensified, sharpened into an ideology, by certain modern anthropologists. A *culture*, as they call it (as though culture, i.e. cultivation, did not imply forethought and purposive effort), is a complex and delicate balance which the clumsy mind and the heavy hands of man could only imperil. Do not disturb it by vain efforts at *progress*. If you deprive a cannibal of his ancestral customs, you undermine the society in which he moves, lives and has his being. You make him a detached individual wandering in a chaotic world.

Here we find the shadow of a contradiction: the obscurantists admit that tradition, although unreasoning, is conscious. Natural functions, like breathing and sleeping, are not traditional. Neither are those instincts probably older

---

[7] The word "obscurantist" is not intended here as a term of reproach. The opponents of the Enlightenment, the worshipers of dark forces, were literally obscurantists.

than mankind: lust, pugnacity, but also love. A tradition exists as such because of our awareness. If the tradition is explained, rationalized, justified, it ceases to be purely a tradition. As soon as you try to demonstrate the wisdom of prejudice, it is no longer prejudice, but judgment.

I submit that sheer inertia, denying the power of human thought and human will, never was the dominant factor in *civilized* society; and that the decline of tradition, in spite of the vigorous counter attacks of the obscurantists, is proceeding under our eyes at a breathtaking pace. The scientific spirit, which is now assuming control, is the denial of tradition. Tradition and the free mind were long engaged in dubious battle; but at no time, even in the high Middle Ages—nowhere, even in China or in that fascinating Old Curiosity Shop, England—was tradition in exclusive control.

Tradition pure and simple is the basis of the Catholic Church. Protestantism rests upon revelation as found in the Scriptures, interpreted by the individual; but it was the Church that gave the New Testament its canonical status. Within the Church, however, the element of thought and energy has always been essential. There were apostles, and there are missionaries, with definite ends in view. There were heretics, exploring the confines of faith, and compelling the orthodox to reach formal decisions, in self-defense or in counterattack. There were religious orders, striving to shape the Church and the world anew. There was—there is—a tremendous philosophical effort, attempting to open the eyes of the faithful, to define the mysteries, to resolve contradictions, to organize religious thought according to a rigorous and lucid method. Thomism is a magnificent attempt to substitute *wisdom* for *prejudice*. There is an abyss between orthodoxy and superstition.

England takes pride, even today, in being a citadel of

tradition. Leave logic to French shallowness, theoretical science to German pedantry: we men of Britain muddle through somehow, through our "congruency with the unutterable." Unthinking has thus reached the status of a national idol. But it is an idol with feet of clay. England has repeatedly muddled into disaster— then rescued herself, magnificently, by cogent thinking and efficient planning. Her age-long safety (until yesterday) was due to her being an island; her lead in the industrial revolution to the abundance and close proximity of coal and iron. But her cultural, political and economic greatness has a deeper cause: the boldness and clarity of her thought.

All the ideas on which the modern, the progessive world is thriving were first focused in England. Bacon sharpened the conception of experimental science and the inductive method. Harvey boldly ignored the "tradition" of Hippocrates and Galen, and established the circulation of the blood. Locke's common sense, i.e. plain reason, illuminated psychology and government. Newton, venturing into strange seas, left traditional authorities far behind. The English deists were the masters of the Enlightenment: Voltaire was England's best gift to France. Adam Smith formulated liberal economics. Malthus posed with almost excessive definiteness the population problem, which today is forcing Japan and India into deliberate action. And although many continental Europeans like Lamarck and Goethe had groped for the concept of evolution, it took an Englishman, Darwin, to bring it into the sharp light of scientific statement.

The British may still decline to challenge obscure rites and customs. The Beefeaters are still on guard at the Tower. Judges still wear (very becoming) wigs. Only yesterday, a member of the House could not resign, but had to apply for the Chiltern Hundreds. A self-respecting statesman must raise prize pigs. But in this delightful Christmas pantomime of Cinque Ports, of Garter and Bath, of Lion and Unicorn, in which Sir Winston had such a glorious time, the English were able to devise and carry out the Beveridge plan, "from the womb to the tomb," and to commit themselves to the welfare state, that bugbear of American conservatives. England may still revere Edmund Burke; but she is taking thought, and using thought as a guide to government.

Not merely in England, but throughout the world, do we see the collapse, the utter dissolution, of tradition as such. No group of men could be more tradition-bound than China, India, Islam: but we have with us the Turkey of Kemal Pasha, the India of Nehru, the China of Mao Tse-tung. The universal rebellion of the retarded peoples against their European masters is a triumph of the radical spirit over tradition. The Europeans, out of respect for native customs (a respect with a Machiavellian tinge) wanted Africa and Indonesia to remain out of the turbulent stream of modern progress. What Ghana and Guinea want is not to revive and preserve tribal superstitions, but to think and act for themselves. They do not wish to be "assimilated," i.e. subjugated, by adopting European traditions: they want to be emancipated through that power of positive thinking and planned endeavor which has made European civilization irresistible.[8]

The key to history therefore is not vegetative growth: it is conscious energy applied to clearly conceived ends. After

---

[8] I do not deny that there is an element of fanatical obscurantism, especially in the case of the Moslems, in that rebellion against Europe. But men like Habib Bourguiba, King Mohammed ben Youssef, and even President Nasser are much closer in spirit to the scientific planners of Europe and the Soviet world than to the blind traditionalists.

all, it was at least six thousand years ago that Adam and Eve nibbled at the forbidden fruit; and thus—*felix culpa!*—arose out of the murk of brutish unthinking into the perilous world of choice and responsibility. Mere tradition is but the flotsam and jetsam of history, not the living stream.

This implies no contempt, or indifference, toward the past. The Parthenon, the Book of Job, the Sainte Chapelle, are not traditions: they are realities for us today. I for one cherish the past because it liberates us from the tyranny of present fashion. We are not allowed to enjoy modern forms of the romantic, the classical or the baroque: the "functional" and the "abstract" are jealous gods, and they have ruthless inquisitors at their service. But we are still able to escape into the past. We would scorn St. Peter's and even the Sainte Chapelle if they were built today: we are permitted to love them because they are old. But they are not vestiges of a vanished world: they are presences.

We are thus led, from the immemorial past, the remembered past, the living past, through the evanescent and illusive present, into the life that is to be. The vital urge is carrying us ever forward; the Golden Age, as Bacon affirmed, lies ahead.

The events chosen by history, *made historical,* are "legends" (i.e. worth reading, worth remembering): those which have impressed themselves upon our minds because of their picturesque and sentimental appeal. The qualities that make them historical are those of the novel and the drama: crisis, surprise, suspense, terror, pity, catharsis. But as in great literature, these events are memorable, beyond mere exciting incidents, because of their significance, of their symbolical value. Thus the mere legend is transmuted into the myth. And myths are of moment to us only as they cast a light upon our life, that is to say upon our future. A myth which does not rouse passionate hope or dread is inert, is dead. Its place is in a dictionary of mythology, not in the minds and hearts of men. Living myths, vital myths, are prospective.

Take the most potent of historical myths, the myth of the nation, illustrated by the legends of the nation: it is the embodiment, not of a memory, but of a hope. There never was a France: there was a growing desire that France should be. The France which five hundred years ago found the formula, "One faith, one law, one king," was in the making: an ideal never to be reached even under Louis XIV. The France, identical and diverse, that proclaimed Liberty, Equality, Fraternity as its *raisons d'être* was and has remained a utopia: jails, compulsory military service, imposed taxes, social and economic classes, civil strife did not disappear. The France prophesied by Hugo, "too great to remain merely a nation," exists only in a few dynamic minds: diplomacy, armies, customs lines, enforced exclusive loyalties, may be on the wane, but they are formidable still. Joan of Arc's career was not a vindication of the shadowy Salic Law, long buried in oblivion. In sober fact, that career was a mere episode, with scant immediate results. It was not the relief of Orléans in 1429 that marked the turning point in the interminable conflict, but the treaty of Arras in 1435. But Joan was the prophetess and the symbol of a great hope, the national monarchy, the intimate union of dynasty and people: a dream which assumed smiling but fugitive definiteness with Henry IV, but which the insane pride of Louis XIV, the bored escapism of Louis XV, the spinelessness of Louis XVI were to dispel altogether. National democracy then took the place of the recusant national monarchy; and in the glowing pages of

Michelet, Joan became not the servant of the king, but the heroine of the people. If nineteenth-century Germany evoked the ghost of Barbarossa, it was not out of sheer antiquarianism: it was as a prophecy of a new Empire. The *Kyffhäuserbund* translated the myth into a principle of action. Again, the vital element in the legend was not the memory, but the hope.

The "land of liberty" which we decreed in 1776 is still struggling to be born. We are creating it—and undoing it—at every step. We are constantly warned that we are straying from the path. And before the American promise is fulfilled, it will assume another shape. Already America is no longer "a mere nation": abjuring parochialism, it is girding itself for "the leadership of the free world"—and leadership means service. This increasing responsibility heralds that "Great Republic of Humanity at large" of which George Washington was proud to call himself a citizen. We are not struggling to preserve unchanged the union of the thirteen colonies: we are the sons and daughters of the *continuous* American Revolution. We are working out its principles; we are fulfilling the past by transcending it. America is not a "tradition," that is to say a fossil, but a utopia.

"If England were but what she seems," sang Kipling, "and not the England of our dreams . . ." The jingo poet was thinking, not of Richard the Lion-Hearted, not of the Virgin Queen, not of Victoria and her sixty years "of ever-expanding commerce," but of a British millennium. In the same way, de Gaulle is not thinking of the splendor once attained by Louis XIV and Napoleon, but of a *grandeur* to be conceived and achieved in the French soul. Lenin knew and proclaimed that the Soviet State was not pure socialism, far less integral communism (which is found only in the religious orders): Russia is struggling through mire and blood, to make a millennium come true. The *myth*, in Georges Sorel's sense of the term, is the asymptote, the constant approach to a state which it will never reach, because the goal itself grows through our very efforts, and beyond our efforts.

Perhaps this conception of the prospective, the creative myth can be most clearly stated in terms of religious history: the will of God made manifest. If we want to reflect on "God in history," we must first brush aside the God of the metaphysicians, absolute, infinite, eternal. Such an abstraction is a mere accumulation of negatives. Its Eternal Present kills the possibility of human growth, freedom, responsibility. It is the denial of history. If He be all, we are nothing. The god of all great faiths is a fighting god, the invisible king under whose banner we serve, to whose service we pledge ourselves. Religion is cosmic drama.

The revolt of the angels, the creation of man, the Fall, the Redemption, are scenes in that immense tragedy. Even purely material catastrophes like the Flood are not chance happenings: they prove the anger and the mercy of God. Now this drama offers, as the very orthodox G. K. Chesterton put it, a tremendous *situation*. It engages our passionate interest because of its *suspense*. The battle is still dubious, for every one of us. And the "far-off divine event" will not be the inevitable happy ending: many are doomed to eternal torment. The catharsis is not yet clear that will reconcile us to such implacable vengeance.

What is real in religion is the promise and the guidance, not the remembrance of things past. It matters little, as the Holy Father himself admitted, whether the world was created six thousand or six billion years ago. What concerns us is our future. In this world, and at once: shall we decide to live henceforth a sober and a godly life? In the world to come: shall we be counted among the saved? The essence of religion, the very nature of faith, is the substance of things hoped for, not vain regrets about the past or smug complacency about the present. We live for that absolute and inconceivable utopia which we call eternal bliss; and for that foretaste of heaven, that purification of mankind before it is absorbed by eternity, which we call the millennium.

Every cause, every faith, every nation, exists only because it heralds a millennium: the man, the community, the Christ that are to be. To write history is to seek justice: historical judgment is a choice between rival millennia. That judgment is moral, not material: Socrates, Jesus, Joan of Arc suffered death, but so did Hitler: victory and defeat are not conclusive arguments. Moses, Caesar, Christ count in history, are part of history, because they affected the course of that Divine Comedy which is in truth the Human Tragedy. History is entrancing because of its suspense. Ineluctable law, whether determinism or predestination, would make history a delusion. At every moment, it might have been, it might yet be, otherwise. It is idle to call this either the best or the worst of all possible worlds: what do we know of such possibilities? It is the world which we refuse to accept, *and* the world we are striving to make: in confusion, in anguish, yet sustained by the faith that the battle is not lost. Every step involves a choice, dictated by a purpose. The task of history is to clarify and purify that purpose. History is not merely the consciousness, but the conscience, of mankind.

Reflections on the Alienation of the Intellectuals

Crane Brinton

I

Crane Brinton was born in Winsted, Connecticut on February 2, 1898. He graduated from Harvard University in 1919 and in 1920 went as a Rhodes Scholar to Oxford University [England], where he received the D.Phil. degree in 1923. In this same year he took up his duties as instructor and tutor at Harvard, becoming a full professor in 1942. Since 1939 he has been a senior fellow of the Society of Fellows, of which he assumed the chairmanship in 1942. During the war, from 1942 to 1945, he served with the United States Army as special assistant, Office of Strategic Services, European Theater of Operations. From 1932 to 1939 he was corresponding secretary of the Harvard chapter of Phi Beta Kappa. In 1946 he married Cecelia Roberts. In 1957–58 he was at the Center for Advanced Study in the Behavioral Sciences at Palo Alto, California.

He holds two L.H.D. degrees, from Ripon College (1951) and from Kenyon College (1952). Among the organizations of which he is a member are the National Institute of Arts and Letters, American Historical Association, the Royal Historical Society, the American Academy of Arts and Sciences and the American Philosophical Society. His books include The Jacobins, English Political Thought in the Nineteenth Century,

A Decade of Revolution, The Anatomy of Revolution, The United States and Britain, From Many One, Ideas and Men, The Temper of Western Europe, The Shaping of the Modern Mind, A History of Western Morals *and* The Fate of Man.

In his suggestive *Natural History of Revolutions* Lyford P. Edwards uses the phrase "transfer of the allegiance of the intellectuals" to describe one element he found common to societies on the eve of major revolutions.[1] When in the early 1930's I was working on the Lowell lectures, which eventually became *The Anatomy of Revolution,* I came across this phrase, and found that the phenomenon it sought to describe fitted in very well indeed with the conceptual scheme of "symptoms" of a coming revolution that was forming in my mind. Perhaps unwisely, however, I shortened and enlivened Mr. Edward's phrase into "desertion of the intellectuals," a term which does indeed seem to carry some weight of condemnation of the deserters.[2] The now current phrase "alienation of the intellectuals" was almost certainly in common use twenty-five years ago. For one thing, the late Julien Benda's *Trahison des clercs,* first published in 1927, was widely read, at least among the *clercs,* throughout the West; and though Benda's *trahison* was neither "desertion" in my sense nor "alienation" as we now fashionably use the term, his *clercs* were indeed our intellectuals.[3]

---

[1] Lyford P. Edwards, *The Natural History of Revolutions* (Chicago, 1927), 38.

[2] Crane Brinton, *The Anatomy of Revolution* (Vintage Books ed., New York, 1957), 44.

[3] The American translation bore the title *The Treason of the Intellectuals* (New York 1928); the Beacon Press paperback edition (Boston, 1955) has the title *The Betrayal of the Intellectuals.* Benda meant by *trahison*—a stronger term than "desertion," surely—what to him was the shocking participation in modern competitive business, entertainment and politics of intellectuals who should have kept themselves

At any rate, however, I did not use the phrase "alienation of the intellectuals" in my book in 1937, and in a revised edition of the book in 1957 I deliberately refrained from adopting what was by that time a very familiar phrase indeed. I now incline to wish that I had gone back to Mr. Edwards's original phrase, smacking a bit of sociological English though it does. For what "transfer of allegiance" does imply is that the intellectuals in these specific situations in history did indeed have allegiances to some specific thing—if only a specific "cause" or "movement" here on earth. The phenomenon I was there studying—one which all students of revolutions, or at least all concerned with the study of comparative history, have noticed—is by no means exactly what is mostly meant nowadays by "alienation of the intellectuals." The two sets of realities behind the phrases are of course related, if only because both refer to the behavior of human beings we group—not, I think, arbitrarily or artificially—as intellectuals. But the behavior of the intellectuals I was concerned with in the study of the great English, French and Russian revolutions of modern times is not exactly the kind of behavior of contemporary Western intellectuals we are concerned with now.

For the seventeenth-century English Puritans and parliamentarians, the eighteenth-century French *philosophes* and the nineteenth-century Russian *intelligentsia* and their followers attacked first of all an actual existing government, and a specific socio-economic structure of power and priv-

---

above the melee, serene in the ivory tower which is their true home, and from which alone their light can properly illumine the world. It should be clear already that our subject is full of difficulties of definition of words, for to Benda the intellectuals were not sufficiently *alienated* from the world of the market place. The fundamental concept of alienation, if not the word itself, suggested to him the normal, the *right* condition of the intellectuals. This is I think by no means the current connotation of the word in the United States.

ilege; and—this is most important—they knew, even the vague and soulful Russians knew, what they wanted in place of what they attacked. They were all, again even the Russians—who were certainly rather more afflicted with a kind of *Weltschmerz* than the others—basically optimistic about human nature, or at least optimistic about the possibility of improving human behavior by the kind of changes they wanted to bring about. Most important, though they certainly thought of themselves as leading the many to a better life, though they displayed toward privileged aristocrats, benighted priests and other opponents strong sentiments of hatred—better, of moral indignation—they did not display such emotions toward all poor ordinary nonintellectual human beings. They were not on the defensive, were not even much disposed to feel martyred, save in a confident way quite different from the way most of us intellectuals felt about our martyrdom during the McCarthy era. They were not, in short, it seems to me, *alienated*.

Yet even if you cannot quite accept the distinction I have been trying to make above, you should be able to admit that the comparative historian of actual and—as far as revolutions ever end—now ended revolutions, has a different set of problems, and therefore is studying a different reality, from the sociologist-publicist-historian concerned with the status, role and morale of an intellectual class or classes in societies not on the eve of revolution. I used in *The Anatomy of Revolution*—with due apologies for its dyslogistic connotations—the conceptual scheme of a fever. Now, though perhaps briefly after the epochal discoveries of Pasteur and his colleagues, the medical profession tended a bit toward too simple and frequent use of "specific etiology"—i.e., belief that a given microbe "causes" a given disease in a given patient—the profession has long been aware that disease is complex, that the same microbes behave differently in different patients, that rarely indeed in diagnosis or prognosis can any *one* sign or symptom be trusted to bear the whole weight of the physician's decision. Nor is the well-trained and conscientious historian addicted to specific etiology, or its equivalent, in his work. We do indeed have all sorts of troubles and disputes about what we usually call "causation," and we do, after acknowledging other "contributory" causes, not infrequently come close to singling out some master cause, usually in the United States a version of that economic interpretation which always asks a naïve *Cui bono?* Certainly we are not nowadays inclined to find the sole cause of the French or any other revolution in the activities of Voltaire, Rousseau and the intellectuals generally.

Those of us who have attempted some study of the comparative history of revolutions have certainly been fully aware of the complexity of their "backgrounds," "causes," "etiologies," or whatever general term you prefer. I still think that the "transfer of allegiance of the intellectuals" in the three revolutions I studied in the 1930's—and to a degree even in the American Revolution, which I used then as a kind of control—is an objective fact, and an important element in any analysis of these revolutions. In all three societies, the intellectuals of a cultural generation or two earlier had been on the whole, in general, other things being equal (I am not being ironic, merely emphatic) loyal to, supporters of, satisfied with, *not the universe, not the whole of things-as-they-are,* but at least with the established order, the "regime." The Elizabethans were proud of state and society, loyal to their queen; from Shakespeare to Milton, transfer of allegiance. The great writers and artists of the age of Louis XIV, before the fistula, seem to most

Americans to have been disgustingly proud of their king and their society; from Boileau to Diderot, transfer of allegiance. The Russians, I admit, are a less clear case, partly because theirs was a culturally backward country almost without an intellectual class until the eighteenth-century Enlightenment was imported.[4] Not even the clergy in old Russia were true intellectuals, for their social position was much too low. Even so, though the first name stands almost alone, one may say from Karamzin to Herzen, transfer of allegiance. Even in New England, to a degree the formula holds: from the Winthrops and the Mathers to the Adamses, transfer of allegiance.

As one variable, then, in the most complex set of variables we may still think of—cautiously—as "causes" of certain modern social, economic and political revolutions, this reasonably easily identifiable attitude of the intellectual classes seems evident enough. Arthur Wilson, indeed, has found a neater example of this *transfer of allegiance* than any I succeeded in dredging up:

In that very year [1749] in which were produced all these great philosophical works, we saw beginning a succession of unfortunate events that little by little and from day to day stripped from the government that public approbation and esteem that up to that time it had enjoyed; and while we passed from the love of belles-lettres to the love of philosophy, the nation, owing to a change explained by causes quite different, passed over from acclamations to complaints, from songs of triumph to the clamor of perpetual remonstrances, from prosperity to fears of

---

[4] One of the most useful recent contributions to the study of revolutions is T. H. von Laue, "Die Revolution von aussen als erste Phase der russischen Revolution 1917" (*Jahrbücher für Geschichte Osteuropas*, IV, 2; Munich, 1956), in which the author points out that the guiding ideas and impulses of the Revolution of 1917 came from outside Russia, from a more "advanced" West.

a general ruin, and from a respectful silence regarding religion to importunate and deplorable quarrels. . . . The capital [Paris], which for so long a time had been the prompt and docile imitator of the sentiments, taste, and opinions of the Court, at the same time ceased to have for the latter its old-time deference. Then it was that there arose among us what we have come to call *the empire of public opinion*. Men of letters immediately had the ambition to be its organs, and almost its arbiters. A more serious purpose diffused itself in intellectual works: the desire to instruct manifested itself in them more than the desire to please. *The dignity of men of letters,* a novel but an accurate expression, quickly became an approved expression and one in common use.[5]

Yet even as in the 1930's I worked over samples of the vast surviving literature of protest and attack in these societies, I was moved to ask myself, Well, isn't most of our literary heritage, at least of the kind time has sealed with greatness, the kind the French call *sérieux,* an attack on something? Reporting without judging is surely rare? And there are no Pollyannas among the great. The song Browning has Pippa sing,

God's in his heaven,
All's right with the world

is a song Browning himself never sang very clearly. In fact, it was the notably censorious attitude of most of the great Victorian intellectuals, including that nay-saying preacher of yea-saying, Thomas Carlyle, that first set my mind reaching beyond the narrow problem of the attitudes of my prerevolutionary intellectuals.[6] Just what, if such exists, is the

---

[5] C.-C. de Rulhière, quoted in A. M. Wilson, *Diderot: The Testing Years* (New York, 1957), 94–95.

[6] I tried briefly in *The Anatomy of Revolution* to come to grips with

normal attitude of the intellectuals toward the universe, their society, their fellow men? Clearly this is a much bigger problem than the one I was originally concerned with, and in large part a different one. It sets in a much more useful framework than do my revolutions the problem we all know so well nowadays as the alienation of the intellectuals.

II

There has been a great deal written in these last few years about the state of mind of the intellectuals, especially in the United States. The subject is a natural one for the serious magazine of opinion in this country. The *Partisan Review* in 1952 published a series on "Our Country and Our Culture" in which twenty-five well-known writers, from both the academic world and the great world of letters, took part. Not inappropriately, perhaps indeed symptomatically, the final installment of the symposium appeared in a number of the magazine with a part of George Orwell's autobiographical essay *Such, Such Were the Joys,* beginning:

---

the difficulties suggested by the apparent desertion—or alienation—of the Victorian intellectuals in a society we know was not in a pre-revolutionary stage. I might have argued that though this desertion or alienation of the intellectuals was *one* revolutionary symptom, the others were lacking, and therefore no revolution. But I felt, and still feel, that the Victorian intellectuals were not in a state of mind and heart like that of the intellectuals in the prerevolutionary societies I was studying. The difference I think is partly one of the Victorian intellectuals' loyalty to the queen and to the political structure; partly of the lack of defined and agreed-upon goals—a lack they share with our intellectuals; partly, and more important, of the non-intellectual habits, traditions, conditioned reflexes of the Victorian intellectuals, which were substantially like those of dull conforming countrymen of theirs. Moreover, there is always among Western intellectuals the disposition to censure. But this is a large subject for a footnote. See my *Anatomy of Revolution* (Vintage Books ed.), 45–47.

Soon after I arrived at Crossgates (not immediately, but after a week or two, just when I seemed to be settling into the routine of school life) I began wetting my bed.[7]

The late lamented *Pacific Spectator* in the last year of its life published a less formally organized but quite as lively series on the place—not quite always on the plight—of the intellectual in the United States. Eugene Burdick kicked off firmly and accurately:

> The intellectual in America is estranged. The fact has been remarked by persons as various as De Tocqueville, Simone de Beauvoir, and Geoffrey Gorer. From what the American intellectual is estranged and to what he is attracted are not so clear. But I, at least, shall not dispute the fact of estrangement.

Albert Guérard, who was inevitably drawn into the ensuing scrimmage, characterized the tone of the other contributors:

> In three consecutive numbers of the *Pacific Spectator, Homo intellectualis* (not *sapiens*) has taken a series of resounding drubbings, and by expert hands. He is "in a plight"; he suffers from "malaise"; he is "psychopathic." [8]

The spiritual condition of *Homo intellectualis* var. *amer-*

---

[7] *Partisan Review*, XIX, 505. The symposium was published in three numbers from May–June through Sept.–Oct. 1952, and reprinted as a single work in 1953 as Symposium Number 4 entitled "America and the Intellectuals". The contributors were Newton Arvin, William Barrett, Jacques Barzun, Louise Bogan, James Burnham, Richard Chase, Allan Dowling, Leslie A. Fiedler, Joseph Frank, Horace Gregory, Sidney Hook, Irving Howe, Louis Kronenberger, Max Lerner, Norman Mailer, Margaret Mead, C. Wright Mills, Reinhold Niebuhr, William Phillips, Philip Rahv, David Riesman, Arthur Schlesinger, Jr., Mark Schorer, Delmore Schwartz, Lionel Trilling.

[8] *Pacific Spectator*, IX, 352; X, 333. In the five numbers of the magazine between the autumn of 1955 and the autumn of 1956 inclusive, the following writers took up the topic: Bruce Bliven, Eugene Burdick, Mary Ann Esser, Leslie Fiedler, Iago Galdston, M.D., Albert Guérard, Eric Hoffer, Russell Kirk, J. D. Koerner, Milton Rose, M.D., Max Savelle.

icanus has come to interest knowing editors of periodicals not usually classified as "serious magazines of opinion," and not commonly limited in circulation to the intellectual classes. *Esquire* in its number for February 1959 published under the title "What Worries You Most About America Today?" the results of an enquiry made in Cambridge, Massachusetts, a town which, in callous disregard of the aspirations to such a title held in a university town a great deal further west of Massachusetts Bay, it calls the "intellectual capital" of the United States. All but one of the intellectuals interviewed confessed their worries, which were high, culture-centered and apparently impersonal. Only one out of the seventeen asserted that he was not worried. In so small a sample, I regard it as quite accidental that this eccentric is a scientist, or at least an engineer; indeed my subjective and quite unstatistically founded impression is that the scientists and the engineers, if not quite as worried as the poets, are still by no means serenely confident that all is well in their world and ours.

The sociologists, cultural anthropologists, behavioral scientists—who, with the exception of a very few such as Margaret Mead and the late C. Wright Mills, do not write for the general magazines, big or little—have in their own media gone to work bravely on the intellectual classes. One whole number of the *Journal of Social Issues* has been devoted to "Anti-intellectualism in the United States"; Edward Shils led off in the first number of a promising learned journal, *Comparative Studies in Society and History,* with an admirable article on "The Intellectuals and the Powers: Some Perspectives for Comparative Analysis"; Dr. G. Nettler has even attempted to measure "alienation," not indeed primarily among "intellectuals," but most certainly with leads from the attitudes of our contemporary intellectuals.[9]

I should not dare attempt a review of the literature of this vast subject here; nor do I intend to make any research soundings of my own. What I should like to do in this brief paper is to suggest some of the difficulties that face the student of human behavior, whether he is historian or contemporary analyst, who is trying to understand the role, status, attitudes and influence of the intellectual classes in any society. Naturally enough, as a historian I am quite sure that no one will get very far in the understanding of the position of the intellectuals in present-day America— or France, or England, or Russia—unless he pushes his studies at least some distance back into the past of the society he is studying; indeed I should go further and argue that only a wide comparative study of the intellectual classes in different times and places will give a sound base for an understanding of their present situation ("plight" seems to me here an avoidable word). At the barest minimum, there is for some of us consolation in realizing that Plato and St. Paul too were alienated.

Many of these difficulties are of course those of definition. The terms we must use cannot be defined as a right-angled triangle can be defined, nor even as *Ulmus americana* can be defined. Both "alienation" and "intellectual" must be used to cover a broad spectrum of different, indeed unique, individuals; and both are liable to stir up even in the very self-conscious social scientist all sorts of sentiments

---

[9] *Journal of Social Issues*, XI (1955); *Comparative Studies in Society and History*, I (1958); G. Nettler, "A Measure of Alienation," *American Sociological Review*, XXII (1957). These are but samples; a few minutes' work in the *Readers' Guide to Periodical Literature* or in the *International Index* under the entry "Intellectuals" will net a surprisingly long list.

that the tradition of scientific investigation considers obstacles to its work. In the rest of us, either term or both can start the adrenal glands into vigorous and obfuscating flow. "Intellectual," for instance, has for many Americans too close a resemblance to "intelligent" and "intelligence," both words suggesting very fine things indeed, not to carry in itself desirable overtones; but when "intellectuals" is used to indicate a small privileged group, the average American feels excluded. He feels sure he is intelligent, but he knows he is not recognized as an intellectual. He feels unjustly excluded.[10]

Moreover, it is at least as difficult to define "intellectual class" in a complex society as it is to define any social or economic class. Is an elementary schoolteacher as such a member of the intellectual class? A university football coach? A surgeon? Is perhaps the term "intellectual" more commonly used even by intellectuals themselves to denote an individual of a certain disposition, as a psychological term, rather than to indicate membership in a class, or status, or vocation—in short, as a sociological term? Here once more I can only pause at difficulties. I shall merely make a few cautious bits of definition, definitions which will involve a very cursory glance at a distant past of Western society.

It seems clear that, oversimple though the dualism may be for close work, there have been for several thousand

---

[10] I cannot get involved in the problem of how the ordinary American feels toward those he has often known as highbrows, longhairs, eggheads. There is surely some envy, and even occasionally a touch of admiration, mixed with the scorn these words carry. See for a fine illustration the letter to the editor signed "Robert Zufall, M.D." in the *New York Times Magazine,* written in furious protest against an article on "The Egghead Looks at Himself" by Professor S. M. Lipset in the same magazine a fortnight earlier. (*New York Times Magazine,* November 17, 1957; December 1, 1957, p. 31).

years in the West two broad kinds of privileged classes—yes, aristocracies—that of the warrior-politician-administrator and that of the priest-intellectual-artist. Even in the Middle Ages, which cherished the distinction between the *vita activa* and the *vita contemplativa,* the two classes were by no means mutually exclusive; on the other hand, not even those splendid lovers of the beautiful-and-good, the Athenians, nor the Renaissance men of *virtù,* quite achieved in their persons a complete union and reconciliation of the two aristocracies. The relations between the two classes, the recruitment of their members, their privileges, almost everything about them, has varied historically a very great deal. In spite of adages like "The pen is mightier than the sword" it has been generally true in the West that the warrior-politician-administrator has ranked first in power, wealth and prestige; though it is also true that for the thousand years of the medieval *Ständestaat* in the West, the clergy were formally registered as the First Estate, the nobles as the Second.

In the earliest medieval centuries, the clergy were the sole intellectuals. Soon, however, as medieval society grew in wealth, orderliness and complexity, the intellectual class was widened to include liberally educated laymen; in the modern world, the clergy are a relatively small part of the class, but a sense of moral and spiritual obligation toward the community, indeed a sense of having cure of souls, remains very strong indeed in most of the class. The other aristocracy too has widened its net greatly in modern times. Notably the man of affairs, or finance, business, entrepreneurship has come to full membership in it. The curious notion widely held among some American intellectual groups that this aristocracy of the *vita activa* in contemporary America is wholly made up of "businessmen" or at least wholly dominated by businessmen, and therefore quite unique in Western history, is simply not true. All the opinion polls show that our modern American equivalents of the Marlboroughs, the Richelieus, the Cokes, the Frederick II's, are ranked well ahead of our equivalents of the Fuggers and the Rothschilds. And among the men of affairs the most highly honored are surely the great Promethean innovators, the magicians of science and invention, Edison, Ford, and the rest, all touched with something of the artist-priest-intellectual.

It is unfortunate, not alone because of the hindering sentiments the term arouses, but because it does not sufficiently point to the essentially priestly character of the class, that we are obliged to retain the term "intellectual class." Coleridge in one of his better prose works tried to use the term "clerisy" for the class:

The Clerisy of the nation, or national Church, in its primary acceptation and original intention, comprehended the learned of all denominations, the sages and professors of the law and jurisprudence, of medicine and physiology, of music, of military and civil architecture, of the physical sciences, with the mathematical as the common organ of the preceding; in short, all the so-called liberal arts and sciences, the possession and application of which constitute the civilization of a country, as well as the theological.[11]

But the word has not caught on in the slightest. Benda clearly meant by his *"clercs"* what Coleridge meant by "clerisy," but even in French the word now has an archaic touch. It would, however, help a bit if we could consistently

---

[11] S. T. Coleridge, *On the Constitution of the Church and State* (Professor Shedd, ed., *Complete Works,* VI [1854], 53).

use, or at least think always of, James Harvey Robinson's "intellectual class"—or classes—instead of plain "intellectuals."

In the intellectual class today in the United States I should include those who teach, preach, do research in the fields of science and learning, write, compose music, pursue the fine arts, and those who regard their role as audience or followers of such persons as the most important or significant part of their lives. I do not, obviously, think the term can be best used as a term limited to description of a calling, profession, or vocation. Some element of attitude, of feeling of belonging to a "clerisy," of the importance of what the clerisy wants and does, must enter in. Thus, the intellectual class—"intellectuals" for short—would not for me be by any means synonymous with the "liberal professions" or the "educated class." Most American physicians, for instance, are not intellectuals; a physician who really wanted to reform American medical practice, or greatly and quickly prolong the average life span, or lift even slightly by his own action the public health of the Burmese —the medical missionary in short—I should regard as an intellectual. But though these last concrete examples all suggest Leftist, or at least humanitarian democratic activities and sympathies, I do not think a member of the intellectual classes in this country *must* be a "liberal." [12] The "new conservatives" of the 1950's, like their predecessors, the "new humanist" followers of Irving Babbitt and the Southern "agrarians" of the 1920's, are most certainly intellectuals. Indeed, I think we have to call Westbrook

---

[12] Incidentally, "liberal" in this country is, as many even of the "liberals" know, another nightmare for the semanticist. Yet it is also another one of those words we all have to use—indeed one of those words that are useful, and to a degree clear, just because they are imprecise.

Pegler, and surely we have to call Lawrence Dennis, an intellectual.

It is, then, worth noting that the intellectual classes are by no means monolithic. There are all sorts of gradations of prestige within the classes, and a great range of actual incomes. There are great variations of attitudes toward politics, morals, "values." It is probably true that the "creative" intellectuals, and in particular those who create through the written or spoken word, are considered both by their noncreative fellow intellectuals and by outsiders to the class as setting the tone, defining the attitudes of the whole class. Yet the relation between this creative minority and the majority of the class is by no means always clear and simple, certainly not an equivalence of attitudes. A degree of what I should define as "high-minded alienation" has certainly in our time prevailed among the intellectual leaders of the class; this alienation is certainly vastly diminished in intensity among most of those who read or listen to these leaders. In other words, the schoolteachers, the earnest and dedicated lady joiners of all sorts of formal and informal lecture-discussion groups, the *homme moyen intellectuel,* are less likely to come close to the model suggested by the sequence highbrow-longhairs-egghead than the university professors or the free-lance writers.

As for "alienation," it too carries unfortunate overtones. Not so very long ago the psychiatrist was for the press at least always an "alienist"; and "alien" remains in this country so unpleasant a way of saying foreigner that Americans landing in Britain have been known to deny that they are aliens there. Yet it is an established word in this context, and there is no great harm in our using it here. After all, only the most hostile or the most pessimistic writing about the state of mind of our American intellectuals seems quite to equate alienation with insanity—or, since this last word too seems on its way out, let us politely say, with a psychopathic condition.

III

For the historian willing to work at this sort of retrospective sociology, there are plenty of interesting and, one hopes, useful opportunities. His source material will not be anything like as abundant as it can be for the analyst of a contemporary society, but he can without seriously damaging his standards as a skilled craftsman do something toward answering a whole set of problems. For any given society, what is the composition of the intellectual class or classes? How much individual social mobility is there within such a class or classes? How do intellectuals make—or get—a living? Can they be divided, along some such lines as those I have suggested above, between the few "creators" and the many "followers" in our American society? What are the relations between the intellectual leaders—or "elites" if you can stand that soiled word—and the other leaders of the society? Can it be justly said of the intellectual leaders, or of the class as a whole, that it is "alienated"? What is the relation between the stability or instability of a given society and the attitudes and functions of its intellectuals?

In particular, I think that closer and more detailed study of the socio-economic position of various kinds of intellectuals, and notably writers, artists and educators in the past, right back to the Greeks and the Jews, would be most rewarding. We know the broad outlines of some of the answers, and we can make big guesses, such as one that the Hebrew prophets were the first "irreconcilable journalists" in part because, at least among the intellectual classes, they were the first to suffer from "technological unemployment." Eric Hoffer, who makes this guess, goes on to explain that the invention of the alphabet made for a sudden increase in the number of literates. These in the Phoenician society in which the invention was made could be absorbed in commerce. But, Hoffer continues,

in the chiefly agricultural Hebrew society the new men of words found themselves suspended between the privileged clique, whose monopoly on reading and writing they had broken, and the illiterate masses, to which they were allied by birth. Since they had neither position nor adequate employment, it was natural that they should align themselves against established privilege, and become self-appointed spokesmen of their inarticulate brethren. Such at least might have been the circumstances at the rise of the earliest prophets—of Amos, the shepherd of Tekoa, and his disciples. They set the pattern; and the road trodden by them was later followed by men of all walks of life, even by Isaiah the aristocrat.[13]

Hoffer, one suspects, loves to shock, and in the great tradition of the Enlightenment loves especially to shock the orthodox, Jew or Christian. I should guess that in the form he gives it, this notion would have seemed a trifle bizarre even to Renan, who gave Hoffer his start on this subject.

It is, however, worth trying to see whether a notion of this sort can be documented. It may be, for instance, that the alienation of our intellectuals today is in part explicable in terms of the relatively new—not much more than two centuries old—dependence of the writer, whether free lance,

---

[13] Eric Hoffer, "The Intellectual Masses," *Pacific Spectator*, X (1956), 8.

or newspaperman, or, though more indirectly, college professor, on the "free" economic choices of the masses in a mass market. In spite of the famous letter of Dr. Johnson to Lord Chesterfield, the noble patron might have been better for the peace of mind of the writer than the patronage of the buyer in the market.[14]

Though all these and many others seem to me worth much more attention from professional historians than they have had, I think the central problems on which we may help throw light for the behavioral scientist concerned with contemporary societies are these: among intellectuals is there a set of normal attitudes toward the society in which they live? If not, is there at least some relation between the nature and extent of dissatisfaction with things-as-they-are (alienation) among intellectuals and the health or stability of their society? Is it possible to establish, if only in the rough, purely "literary" way the humanist has always put his generalizations, some *measure* of the alienation of an intellectual class?[15]

Any answer to these master questions must in my opin-

---

[14] If the reader will forgive a cautionary footnote on method, I really meant the phrase "*in part* explicable." In problems like these, one-way causation, which can explain perhaps the course of a specific billiard ball in a specific game, is much worse than useless. We always deal with something like what the pathologist calls a syndrome. As I have noted above, even the medical profession, which has a long tradition of paying attention to as many of the variables as seemed pertinent, fell under the influence of the great discoveries of Pasteur and his colleagues in the last century, into the bad habit of finding a "specific etiology" for all cases of a disease attributable to a known microbe. On this see the very suggestive René Dubos, *The Mirage of Health* (New York, 1959).

[15] I would not be taken to discourage altogether the attempt to use the kind of statistical techniques of measurement that the behavioral scientists are developing for their use, and which among economists are sophisticated indeed; but I think the sources the historian can use, even for modern history up to a few decades ago, will permit no more than very simple statistical techniques.

ion start with the admission that in the Western tradition something that can be called partial alienation is almost a constant of the intellectual life. The point does not need to be labored. The writer in our tradition does indeed, and not infrequently, describe or report without judging; he sometimes, though less frequently than some literary critics maintain, tells a story with no intent to do more than interest or amuse, sings a song of pure joy or of pure, unalienating sorrow; he sometimes, as we are told of an Edgar Guest or a Samuel Smiles, comes close to praising uncritically things-as-they-are. The painter, the musician, the architect in their own work may indeed seem not directly concerned with human behavior; yet a moment's thought will show that painting as the servant of Christianity—or, notably with those famous Mexicans, as servant of Dialectical Materialism—has a direct part in making a series of judgments or comments on human behavior. And at least in modern times—witness the *Davidsbündler* of romantic Germany—the artists and musicians tend to make as critics of things-as-they-are common cause with the literary.

On the degree of this high-minded alienation, as on its part in social equilibrium, we are reduced to near platitudes, and to dispute at the level of platitudes—or at the very least, we are reduced to metaphors and analogies which come very far from satisfying the devotees of scientific rigor. Is the normal, the essential role of these intellectuals in the West that of the exhorter, the preacher, the Socratic gadfly? Have they in our societies a kind of antiseptic function, and like all psychologically effective antiseptics, must they be rather on the harsh and disagreeable side? Would we all fall shy of what decency we attain if the intellectuals did not tell us how indecent we tend to be? Are the intellectuals spiritual phagocytic white corpuscles which fasten on the microbes of our moral illnesses and the debris of our moral regressions, and keep us in what moral health we have?

I find such concepts offensive to some of my strongest sentiments, but I am prepared to admit that the moralist has here a point. Yet even granting that Socrates, or better Socrates-Plato, set a sound pattern for Western intellectuals ever since, I tend to agree with those who see in the current attitudes of American intellectuals a pushing to extremes of attitudes traditional among intellectuals in the West. The antiseptic nowadays seems too harsh, acidulous in the literary sense of that word. I should not go quite so far as to suggest, following my last metaphor above, that these benign white corpuscles have turned malignant, and that we now are threatened with national spiritual leukemia. Our body politic and moral seems to be far too soundly proof against what the intellectuals do or say.

And yet the suspicion will not quite down: what the writers, the artists, the preachers, the teachers, the leaders who set the fashions, the leaders who in fact lead, are and do is sooner or later, to a degree, followed. If they are not so followed, at least at a distance, I suggest that the whole society of which they form a part is perhaps abnormal, perhaps unstable, perhaps endangered. I should therefore in conclusion like to consider somewhat more specifically some ideas as to how our American—and perhaps indeed our Western—intellectuals came to their present state of mind.

But first, I must admit that the condition I, like a true contemporary intellectual, have been complaining about, perhaps preaching about, may well be in part self-correcting. There are signs in the periodicals the intellectuals themselves write and read that some intellectuals are beginning to revolt—an alienation from the alienated. Here is James Reston in the *one* American newspaper a civilized person can read—well, there are a few others, such as the blessed *Washington Post,* and the *Christian Science Monitor,* but no more than you can count on your fingers. I quote this lively piece at deserved length:

> In this week's New Yorker Magazine there is a cartoon of an angry bartender saying to a customer on the other side of the bar: "Look, my friend, one more comparison between our civilization and Ancient Rome's and out you go!"
>
> This helps a little, for in recent weeks we have been told by everybody from Adlai Stevenson to former Senator William Jenner of Indiana that we are sick and soft and going merrily to hell.
>
> What Oswald Spengler in Germany, "The Gloomy Dean" Inge in England, Peter Drucker in Austria and Nikolai Berdyaev in Russia said of Europe in the Thirties, an odd, mixed-bag of liberal intellectuals, right-wing politicians and retired generals is beginning to repeat about America.
>
> We are, they say, living in a demented world, and ducking our responsibilities. As Berdyaev put it better than the modern Cassandras: there is something shaken and shattered in the soul of modern man. We are entering the realm of the unknown and unlived, joylessly and without much hope. We are now in a time of spiritual decadence, of loneliness and dereliction.
>
> The criers of havoc have always been interesting in every age, and they have often been right. Moreover, they have something to say to us today about the dangers of easy education, free, endless idiot-box entertainment, cheap booze, high wages for sloppy work and early casual marriage. But is this a fair indictment? [16]

---

[16] *New York Times,* Feb. 8, 1959, p. 8 E. And see also Morris Freedman, "The Dangers of Nonconformism," *American Scholar,* XXVIII, Winter (1958–1959); also Saul Bellow, "Deep Readers of the World, Beware!" *New York Times Book Review,* Feb. 15, 1959, p. 1. These examples can be easily multiplied, though they do not yet set the tone for our intellectuals, and perhaps never will.

Mr. Reston goes on to insist that in foreign affairs, for example, our national conduct since the last great war has clearly not been that of a decadent nation. We still, he says, show capacity for moral as well as physical growth. And it is just possible that some day a significant number of the intellectuals will recognize the struggles and disorders of our times as signs of development, as growing pains, as they already do for the sixteenth century, a period in comparison with which ours is almost irenic.

IV

For the present, however, I must agree with Eugene Burdick: the leaders, the creative groups of the American intellectual class are indeed estranged. They are probably rather more estranged than were their predecessors of the naughty and unhappy 1890's. To test this statement, run through a few copies of the *Atlantic Monthly* or *Harper's Magazine* in the 1890's and then compare with them a few of the current issues of these same hardy periodicals. For one thing, you will find in the 1890's a great many ruminative, relatively uncomplaining old-fashioned "essays" and articles that merely inform and explain. Today, almost every piece might be entitled "What's the matter with . . ." The essay, a quiet, reflective, somewhat self-satisfied genre, is dead, killed by worry.

To test the contemporary alienation itself is even simpler: pick a few current numbers of the *New York Times Book Review,* which takes pride in giving a *compte rendu,* real information about what is inside a book, and check off the number of those books, fiction and nonfiction, which to judge from these accounts seem to show no trace of complaining, bellyaching, high-minded alienation. A very random and unsystematic sampling of this sort, which I did in the last few weeks of 1958 and which I should not defend as a social scientist, but which is an approximation to a first approximation, gave me less than 25 per cent as not complaining.[17]

This estrangement, this alienation, is indeed a syndrome. Here I can do no more than to suggest, without any attempt to rank or weigh them, some of the causal factors that may have gone into the making of the syndrome. First of all, even the intellectual, who like myself complains about the complaining intellectuals, has to admit that ours is indeed a Time of Troubles, that, to distribute the moral plague spots with some evenness, names like Belsen, Hiroshima, Katyn Forest, Budapest, Little Rock, Harlem and Havana by no means suggest imaginary evils. The fearful possibilities of what another World War might mean for all humanity are in themselves quite enough to explain why all of us must live with a background of cosmic worries.

But the phenomenon of the alienation of the intellectuals is far older than the potential horrors of the atomic bomb and biological warfare; genocide is far from being as new as its name; and judicial murder is as old as Socrates. There have been many other Times of Troubles. Indeed, it would be well worth while for historians, even if they had to give up their individual independence and take part

---

[17] Here, for example, is a really remarkable specimen of a still fashionable literary and philosophic genre, the historicist prophecy of doom. Miss Hannah Arendt, whose *The Human Condition* (Chicago, 1959), is reviewed by Brand Blanshard in an agreeably skeptical but not unkindly tone, reads Western history from the great Greeks on as a gradual inversion from the delightful free interchange of thoughts and feelings among peers to menial labor to universal slavery, from the beautiful-and-good to *homo faber* to *animal laborans*. She concludes: "It is quite conceivable that the modern age—which began with such an unprecedented and promising outburst of human activity—may end in the deadliest, most sterile passivity history has ever known." (*New York Times Book Review*, Feb. 15, 1959, p. 26.)

in joint research, to test for various societies over the last few millennia just what the relation between bad times and the attitudes of intellectuals may be. Would the work of Thucydides, Plato, even Xenophon have been quite different had Athens won the Peloponnesian War and gone on to flourish? What would Virgil and Livy have written had Rome been badly beaten by Carthage? Yet no clear correlation is obvious, on the surface at least, between the moral as well as physical flourishing of a society and the cheerfulness, self-confidence, optimism of its intellectuals. As I have already suggested, the instance of the Italian Renaissance, when—as a glance at, for instance, the diary of Luca Landucci will make evident—murder, rape, plague, all the catalogue of cruelty and violence was at least as bad as ours, is in itself enough to refute any simple formula for the relation between intellectuals and the society.[18] For I should take it that few historians would call the intellectuals of the Renaissance estranged or alienated in anything like the sense we nowadays give these words.

The problem of correlation between the attitude of the creative intellectuals and the general condition of their society suggests that we are here, like the economic historian and indeed that suspicious character, the philosopher of history, dealing with what has to be called a kind of cycle. The total "culture," in the shaping of which clearly the intellectuals have a major part, of a society, a city-state, a nation, does have its peaks and its troughs—or rather, seems to be a composite of cycles, and for the various arts, music, painting and the like, indeed for that supposedly

---

[18] Luca Landucci, *A Florentine Diary* (English translation, New York, 1947). The entries for the year 1500 will do as a sample. The reading should diminish any romantic desire in the reader to go back to that golden age.

self-winding activity, science, a series of subcycles, which we have hardly begun to understand.[19]

One factor in this cyclical development of culture seems to be directly germane to our present problem. This is the "revolt of the generations," a phenomenon especially clear in the West of the last two centuries. The "cultural generation" is clearly of no neat thirty years' length, nor indeed at all closely tied to a biological generation. But the facts are clear enough: The first romantic generation of the early nineteenth century could not damn their enlightened Voltairean predecessors harshly enough; we who came of age in time to welcome Mencken could not be more scornful of our stuffy, prudish, repressed and repressing Victorian predecessors. In France, Léon Daudet, who was hardly one of us, but was certainly an intellectual, wrote a book he entitled *Le stupide 19me siècle*.

Now I suggest that, especially in the United States, the intellectuals are still, in mid-twentieth century, in self-conscious revolt against the nineteenth century, century of hope, optimism and gentility. The younger ones are no doubt also in revolt against us older ones, but this is no more than a subsidiary revolt. It looks as though the revolt of the cultural generation had been stepped up, intensified, so that there has been a kind of compulsion to repudiate one's master, even when he was a *cher maître* indeed. I should guess this compulsion is in part due to the eternal need for the creative intellectual to be original, to "add" to the fund of culture, a need exacerbated in the scholar,

---

[19] On this matter Spengler, Sorokin, Toynbee and the rest of the philosophers of history are all interesting and suggestive. The work of A. L. Kroeber in this field seems to me, however, almost the only such work to adhere to the traditional standards of the Western scientist. See especially his *Configurations of Culture Growth* (Berkeley, 1944) and his general book *Anthropology* (New York, 1948).

humanist and artist by the acclaim and apparent ease with which their scientific colleagues achieve it.[20] But beyond this compulsion to repudiate one's intellectual fathers lies the cumulative effect of years of criticism of the earlier cultural synthesis. I suggest, then, as a second factor in the attitudes of our contemporary intellectuals that, like the Victorian Samuel Butler, they are still fighting a father-image—the same one he fought.

A third factor applies particularly to the large and important segment of the intellectual class concerned with the arts and with scholarship, in contrast to those concerned with science and technology. Now it is precisely these people, and especially the writers, the columnists, the preachers, the teachers, all those concerned as *politiques et moralistes* with what amounts to cure of souls, who set the moral tone of the class. For these people, both in and out of academic life, the rapid rise of the natural scientists and engineers to the top of the pecking order has been hard indeed to bear. It is clear that among the now large educated general public in the West the nuclear physicist has the place once occupied by the man of God, and in the Enlightenment by the man of letters. We have almost reversed the order of rank so nicely displayed in the academic procession of the classic German university—black-clad theologians in the lead; lawyers, physicians, philosophers and the other members of the liberal professions in appropriate colors following; vulgar scientists, left only some ambiguous shades, ending the procession. Such a transvalua-

---

[20] A fine example of this revolt of the generations is R. O. Rockwood, ed., *Carl Becker's Heavenly City Revisited* (Ithaca, 1958), a symposium in which a number of historians, many of whom were Becker's own pupils, tore apart on the twenty-fifth anniversary of its publication the master's *Heavenly City of the Eighteenth-Century Philosophers* (New Haven, 1932).

tion of values is naturally enough hard for those downgraded to bear. Some of the complaints and worries of our intellectuals spring directly from this social downgrading, and express themselves in "antiscientism"; more of their complaints simply work over into a general conviction that the times are out of joint.

A fourth factor, like the preceding, must be listed among the less noble, if for the hard-boiled analyst realistic enough, of these driving sentiments among our intellectuals. A most pertinent question in any study of alienation is, alienation from what, or whom? There seem to be times, certainly in the history of Christianity, when some very distinguished intellectuals are most eloquently and movingly alienated from the whole of this world, from all classes, from all ways of life, from all but God, who demands of the true believer such alienation. This is the alienation—not in my opinion pathological—that made many a Christian saint. But I cannot feel that even our most distinguished existentialists are quite so transcendentally, so nobly, alienated. And for most of our intellectuals, the question, alienation from what or whom must be thus answered: from the many, from the vulgar, from the bourgeois—and the proletariat.

The honeymoon between the intellectuals and the many which we call the Enlightenment, in which clearly the intellectuals were the admired and loving male, ended for many with the French Revolution. For a while, some of the intellectuals could decide that though the bourgeois were hopelessly corrupted, the people, workmen or peasants, were sound at heart. The Russian Revolution, and the earlier fascist ones, made this belief difficult for all but the very few enthusiasts. It began to seem that evil here on earth is not the product of a few villains—kings, nobles, priests, the rich—but something almost as deeply set in human beings of all sorts—save the intellectuals—as the Christian docrine of original sin implies. This conclusion carried with it an obvious corollary, most important for us today. The intellectuals of the eighteenth century, and even to a degree of the nineteenth, knew what they wanted; they had a program; they wanted *true* democracy. The Marxists carried this conviction down into our own time. But in mid-twentieth century, it is clear that the intellectuals for the most part do not know the good arrangements, institutions, beliefs—not even the "ism"—they want to put in place of existing evil ones.[21]

For American intellectuals, trust and even love for the common man was stronger and has proved more enduring than among their European counterparts. Nevertheless, it has become increasingly difficult for American intellectuals to blame Wall Street, Hollywood, even Rotary, for the failure of our society to resemble what the intellectuals felt should be the Good Society. Or rather, when they began to blame Rotary, or the "businessman" or the Babbitts, it began to dawn on them that they were blaming, not a few privileged villains, but most of their countrymen. All sorts of evidence has been piling in to make them feel that a lot has gone wrong. The educated many turn not to Plato, nor Thoreau, nor John Dewey, but to the horrors of Westerns, comics, cheesecake and gore.

---

[21] This lack of a firm positive program, even in politics, is surely a major reason why the alienation of American intellectuals today is not a "transfer of allegiance," not a symptom of possible revolutionary action in our society, the kind of symptom I considered at the very beginning of this essay; and this lack is also a major reason—peace to A. M. Schlesinger, Jr.—why the state of mind of our intellectuals in 1932 was no sign of a coming revolution, a coming which has hardly threatened, or promised, in the slightest in our perhaps all-too-stable American society.

I need not insist on the obvious. It will be more useful to note here two corollaries to this proposition. First, the intellectual who succeeds in Madison Avenue, Hollywood, Broadway, or even writes a best-seller or produces a popular comic strip, is peculiarly liable to acute attacks of conscience which may break down his health, and always make him a torn soul, neither half of which is very close to the tradition of the beautiful-and-good. Second, even those intellectuals whose success is limited to a *succès d'estime* among their own kind, or who have no success, are subject to this divided state, which I once more do not think quite pathological enough to be called even in metaphor schizophrenia. For they feel they should, as good democrats, as good children of the eighteenth century, love the common people; and in fact they fear and despise them.[22]

This feeling, common among American intellectuals, of fear and contempt for their nonintellectual countrymen, brings me to my final factor. As a result of again many and complex causes, the active, creative, Western intellectuals in very great majority had come by the eighteenth century to have very high hopes indeed for the future—the immediate future, just around the corner. I have elsewhere at some length gone into this aspect of that extraordinary phase of Western culture we call the Enlightenment. Let me summarily put the matter as clearly as possible: a good many enlightened intellectuals came to hold that a heaven on earth is possible soon, a utopian state of human per-

---

[22] Once more, let me point out that I am generalizing, perhaps too sweepingly, but surely not without some basis. I am not asserting anything at all about each and every person in this country who could be assigned membership in the intellectual classes. I am sure there are among our intellectuals lovers of their fellow men, lay saints, as well as honest, well-meaning children of the Enlightenment. I admit I tend to regard these latter as somewhat retarded children.

fectibility which at its height in the work of Condorcet took the almost incredible form of a suggestion that individual disease-free immortality in this flesh here on earth is the true end of man.[23] The intellectuals, even if they went by no means as far as Condorcet, did come as a whole to expect a lot more of this earthly life, the only life they felt they could have—to expect a lot more of themselves, and of the rest of mankind. Realization of that expectation surely seems no nearer in 1963—I should guess it quite safe to say, seems much farther off—than in 1763. Our intellectuals are having a much harder time adjusting themselves to the failure of their eschatological concept—which I shall call the belief in a First and Final Coming of their god, Nature-Reason—than the early Christians had in accepting the indefinite postponement of their expectation of a Second Coming of Christ. Right now they are in a particularly difficult phase of that adjustment, for like the early Christians, they had firmly expected to make a much more pleasant one, and soon. No wonder they are alienated.

I have throughout this essay avoided the difficult task of sorting out the *kinds* of alienation shown in the writing of our contemporary American intellectuals. The determined classifier would have to have a large number of categories, from prophets of varied dooms through many purely neurotic worriers, to Machiavellians, like their master mostly idealists *à rebours,* innocent nature lovers, innocent planners, even more innocent social psychologists, unprincipled idealists and on almost, but not quite, to genuine transcendentalists and mystics. He would have to classify a range of tone from the bitterest of verbal—but still adrenal—fury to near serenity, with a wistful irony, *New Yorker*

---

[23] See my *History of Western Morals* (New York, 1959), especially Chap. XI.

fashion, somewhere near the median. Our courageous taxonomist of *Homo intellectualis,* who, as Albert Guérard noted, has to be himself an intellectual, might well feel obliged to come to the conclusion that one of the great complaints of our kind, that Americans think, feel, hope, *are* alike, most certainly does not apply to our intellectuals.

I have also, not wholly unintentionally, emphasized the less lofty explanations for the present state of mind of American intellectuals. There is no doubt in them, as in all human beings, envy, pride, selfishness, backbiting, cruelty; and there is, perhaps, since they are so bright, even more skillful self-deception among them than among their less gifted fellows; they find it easy to be nobler than they are. But they often are indeed noble. I should not like to end on a note of sourness. The American intellectual shares to the full the great American dream, the hope of the brotherhood of men undivided by evil. He wants us all to be free, happy, virtuous, uninvidiously equals. The ethical quality of these ideals is—unless you are a strictly orthodox Christian—as lofty as that of the early Christians.

But the early Christians had to adjust to the postponement of their millennium; our intellectuals have not yet adjusted to the postponement of theirs, which we now call with St. Thomas More a "no-place." There may be signs— I think there are—that such an adjustment is slowly being made. Even existentialism, atheistic as well as pseudo-Christian, though on the surface it may look like just more alienation, is perhaps one such sign. The success of a writer like Toynbee is another such sign; so too is the prestige of a Reinhold Niebuhr among the young, and indeed so too is the sometimes overestimated but real "return to religion." So, even, is some of the current of thought the still innocent children of the Enlightenment like to call anti-intellectualism—including, in its total influence, the work of Freud and indeed much of modern psychology and even of modern sociology and cultural anthropology. Freud has almost succeeded in convincing our intellectuals that evil is as "natural" as is good in nature and in human nature. Not bleakly, not even wistfully, perhaps indeed not at all in the mood in which he wrote it, we may say with Robert Frost that the intellectuals are learning what to make of a diminished thing.

And yet——what we see thus diminished is nothing as simple as a summer, and the atomic bomb seems a more ominous symbol than the poet's ovenbird. What is diminishing for the high-minded intellectuals is a hope, an ideal, a faith, and perhaps one that may not stand much diminution. There are those who hold that if we do not believe that we must and can make this earth a heaven, it will not even be a hell for long. These are indeed the alienated, well beyond any therapy of ours.